Editor
Mary S. Jones

Managing Editor
Karen J. Goldfluss, M.S. Ed.

Cover Artist
Barb Lorseyedi

Art Production Manager
Kevin Barnes

Imaging
Ricardo A. Martinez

Publisher
Mary D. Smith, M.S. Ed.

Practice Makes Perfect Puzzles
GRADE 4

Author

Mary Rosenberg

Teacher Created Resources, Inc.
6421 Industry Way
Westminster, CA 92683
www.teachercreated.com

ISBN-1-4206-3909-9

©2006 Teacher Created Resources, Inc.

Made in U.S.A.

Teacher Created Resources

Table of Contents

Introduction. 3

Puzzle 1: Rounding Numbers 4

Puzzle 2: What's the Number? 5

Puzzle 3: Comparing Five-Digit Numbers 6

Puzzle 4: Comparing Six-Digit Numbers 7

Puzzle 5: Can You Find It? 8–9

Puzzle 6: All in Order! 10–11

Puzzle 7: Name That Shape! 12–13

Puzzle 8: Time for Trivia 14–15

Puzzle 9: Let's Get Adding! 16

Puzzle 10: Adding to the Hundred Thousands 17

Puzzle 11: You Do the Math! 18

Puzzle 12: More Subtraction Practice 19

Puzzle 13: Subtraction in the Millions 20

Puzzle 14: Extra Practice with Adding and Subtracting 21

Puzzle 15: What's Missing? 22

Puzzle 16: Multiplying by One Digit 23

Puzzle 17: Multiplying Multiple Digits. 24

Puzzle 18: Multiplication by Tens. 25

Puzzle 19: Multiplying by 10, 11, 12, and 13 26

Puzzle 20: Multiplication Challenge 27

Puzzle 21: Prime Time. 28

Puzzle 22: Division Practice 29

Puzzle 23: Division of Five-Digit Numbers 30

Puzzle 24: The Event. 31–32

Puzzle 25: The Top Ten at the Music Store. 33–34

Puzzle 26: Fireworks for Sale! 35–36

Puzzle 27: Can I Get My Change? 37–38

Puzzle 28: Money "Cents" 39–40

Puzzle 29: Tax Time 41–42

Puzzle 30: What's the Amount? 43

Answer Key 44–48

Introduction

The old adage "practice makes perfect" can really hold true for your child and his or her education. The more practice and exposure your child has with concepts being taught in school, the more success he or she is likely to find. For many parents, knowing how to help your children can be frustrating because the resources may not be readily available. As a parent it is also difficult to know where to focus your efforts so that the extra practice your child receives at home supports what he or she is learning in school.

This book has been designed to help both parents and teachers reinforce basic math skills. *Practice Makes Perfect* reviews basic math skills for children in grade 4. This book contains number puzzles that allow children to learn, review, and reinforce basic math concepts. While it would be impossible to include all concepts taught in grade 4 in this book, the following main objectives are reinforced through practice exercises:

- addition
- comparing numbers
- division
- money
- multiplication

- naming shapes
- place value
- rounding
- standard form
- subtraction

There are 30 puzzles organized sequentially, so children can build their knowledge from more basic skills to higher-level math skills. Number puzzles are designed for students to review math concepts and have fun practicing them.

How to Make the Most of This Book

Here are some useful ideas for optimizing the practice pages in this book.

- Set aside a specific place in your home to work on the practice pages. Keep it neat and tidy with materials on hand.

- Set up a certain time of day to work on the puzzles. This will establish consistency. An alternative is to look for times in your day or week that are less hectic and conducive to practicing skills.

- Keep all practice sessions with your child positive and constructive. If the mood becomes tense, or you and your child are frustrated, set the book aside and look for another time to practice with your child.

- Help with instructions if necessary. If your child is having difficulty understanding what to do or how to get started, work through the first problem with him or her.

- Review the work your child has done. This serves as reinforcement and provides further practice.

- Pay attention to the areas in which your child has the most difficulty. Provide extra guidance and exercises in those areas. Allowing children to use drawings and manipulatives, such as coins, tiles, or flash cards, can help them grasp difficult concepts more easily.

- Look for ways to make real-life applications to the skills being reinforced.

Puzzle 1

Rounding Numbers

Round each number. Write each answer in the number puzzle.

Across

2. Round 849 to the nearest hundred. _____

6. Round 29,619 to the nearest ten thousand. _____

7. Round 161,270 to the nearest hundred thousand._____

8. Round 108,615 to the nearest hundred thousand._____

11. Round 71 to the nearest ten._____

12. Round 38,630 to the nearest ten thousand. _____

13. Round 830,445 to the nearest hundred thousand._____

14. Round 29,219 to the nearest ten thousand. _____

15. Round 638 to the nearest hundred. _____

Down

1. Round 7,895 to the nearest thousand._____

3. Round 2,125 to the nearest thousand._____

4. Round 25 to the nearest ten._____

5. Round 43 to the nearest ten._____

6. Round 321,644 to the nearest hundred thousand._____

8. Round 5 to the nearest ten._____

9. Round 386 to the nearest hundred._____

10. Round 59,610 to the nearest ten thousand._____

11. Round 7,085 to the nearest thousand._____

12. Round 3,747 to the nearest thousand._____

13. Round 849 to the nearest hundred. _____

Puzzle 2

What's the Number?

Write each sum in standard form and complete the number puzzle.

Across

1. 400,000 + 7,000 + 300 + 10 + 7 = _____

3. 400,000 + 60,000 + 6,000 + 900 + 6 = _____

7. 400,000 + 90,000 + 8,000 + 40 + 1 = _____

8. 900,000 + 10,000 + 3,000 + 100 + 70 + 1 = _____

9. 700,000 + 30,000 + 9,000 + 500 + 90 + 6 = _____

12. 200,000 + 40,000 + 4,000 + 600 + 80 + 2 = _____

14. 500,000 + 70,000 + 3,000 + 900 + 80 = _____

16. 100,000 + 30,000 + 8,000 + 300 + 90 + 5 = _____

17. 200,000 + 50,000 + 100 + 30 + 4 = _____

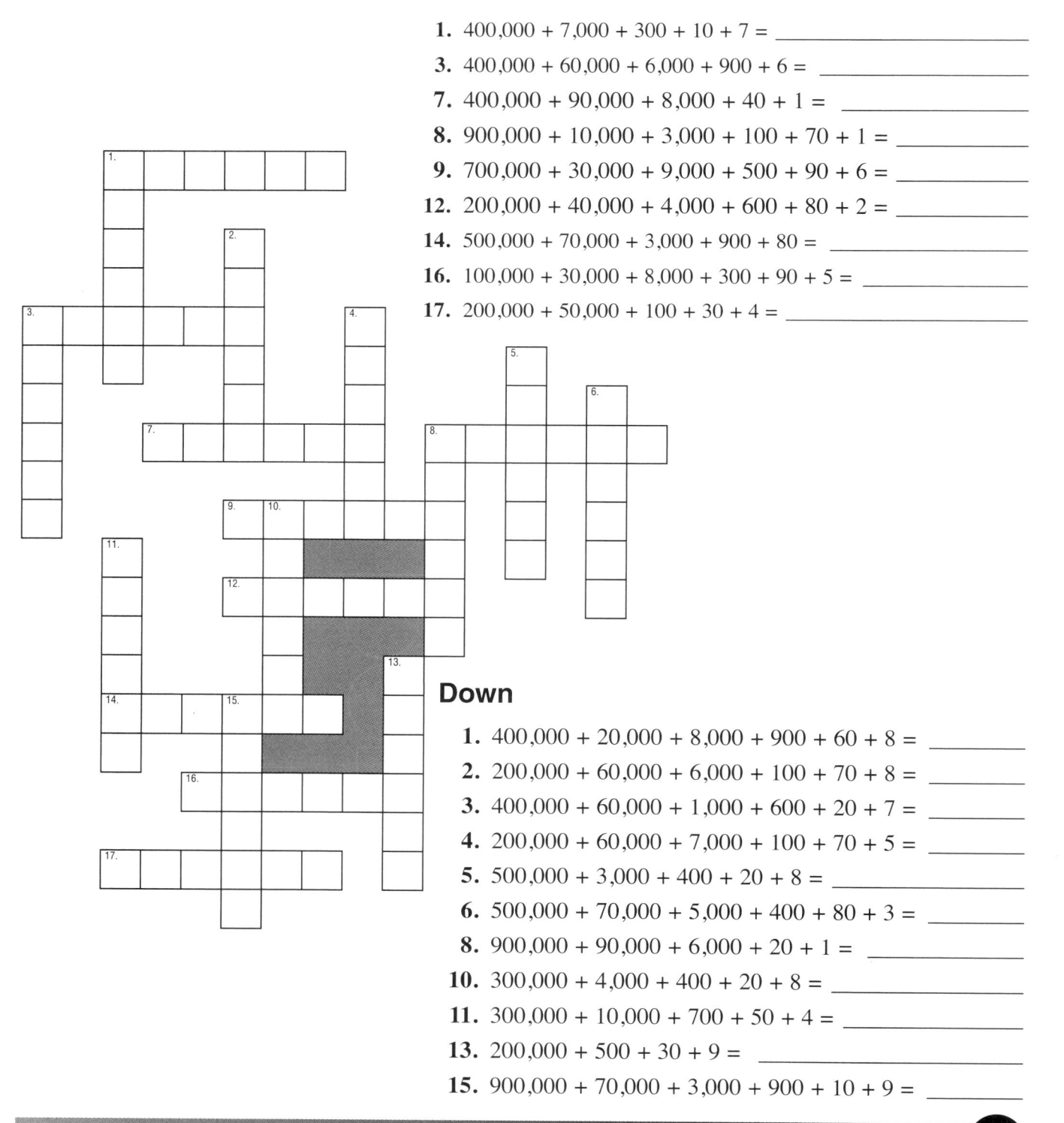

Down

1. 400,000 + 20,000 + 8,000 + 900 + 60 + 8 = _____

2. 200,000 + 60,000 + 6,000 + 100 + 70 + 8 = _____

3. 400,000 + 60,000 + 1,000 + 600 + 20 + 7 = _____

4. 200,000 + 60,000 + 7,000 + 100 + 70 + 5 = _____

5. 500,000 + 3,000 + 400 + 20 + 8 = _____

6. 500,000 + 70,000 + 5,000 + 400 + 80 + 3 = _____

8. 900,000 + 90,000 + 6,000 + 20 + 1 = _____

10. 300,000 + 4,000 + 400 + 20 + 8 = _____

11. 300,000 + 10,000 + 700 + 50 + 4 = _____

13. 200,000 + 500 + 30 + 9 = _____

15. 900,000 + 70,000 + 3,000 + 900 + 10 + 9 = _____

Puzzle 3

Comparing Five-Digit Numbers

Read each clue and compare the numbers. Then, circle the answer and write that number in the number puzzle.

Across

1. Which is larger?   72,975 or 76,151
5. Which is smaller?   26,899 or 28,283
7. Which is smaller?   89,134 or 83,637
8. Which is larger?   10,041 or 10,007
11. Which is larger?   53,537 or 51,286

12. Which is larger?   54,665 or 55,022
13. Which is larger?   40,372 or 42,995
14. Which is smaller? 41,725 or 44,824
15. Which is smaller? 60,377 or 60,546
16. Which is larger?   38,465 or 37,246
18. Which is larger?   95,888 or 99,230

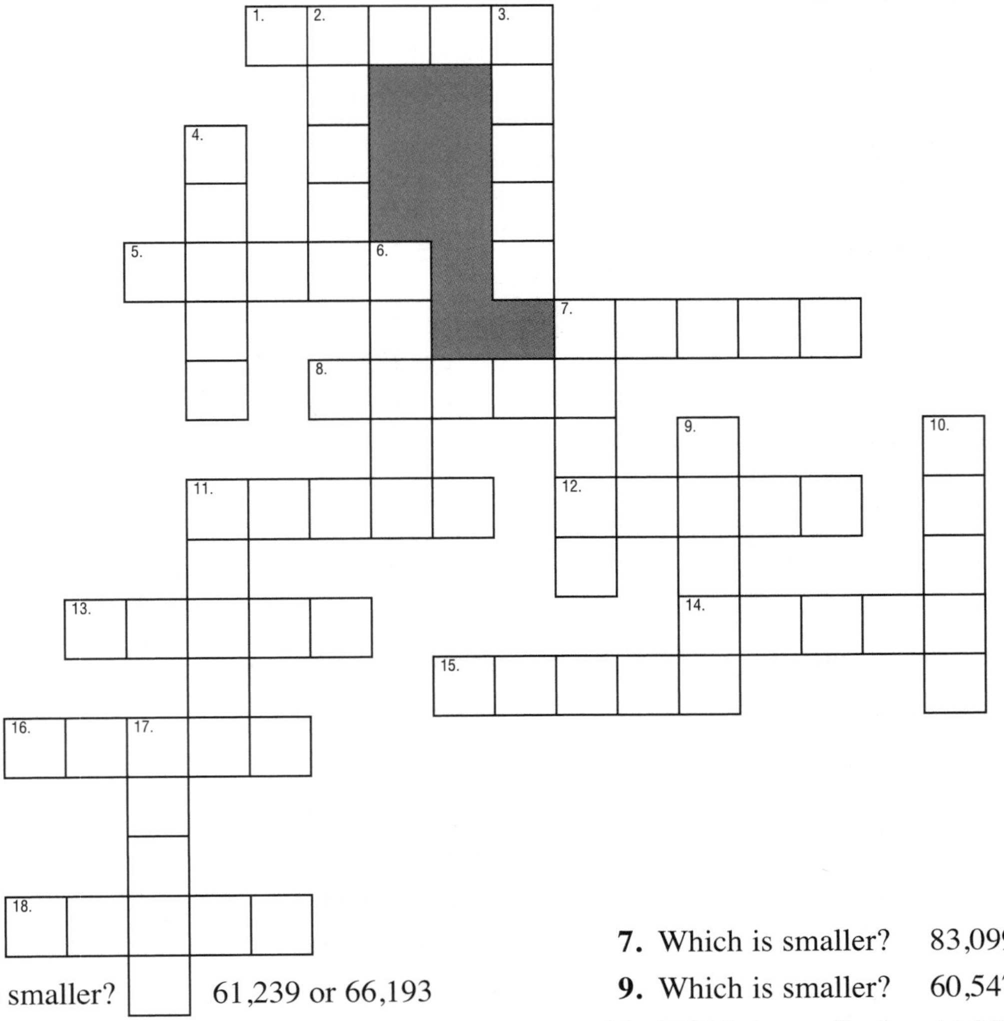

Down

2. Which is smaller?   61,239 or 66,193
3. Which is larger?   19,512 or 13,372
4. Which is larger?   93,774 or 94,670
6. Which is larger?   91,260 or 95,063

7. Which is smaller?   83,099 or 81,359
9. Which is smaller?   60,547 or 68,205
10. Which is smaller? 44,252 or 49,468
11. Which is larger?   57,203 or 58,926
17. Which is smaller? 41,725 or 44,824

Puzzle 4

Comparing Six-Digit Numbers

Read each clue and compare the numbers. Then, circle the answer and write that number in the number puzzle.

Across

2. Which is smaller?   916,367 or 982,081

6. Which is smaller?   198,399 or 147,956

7. Which is larger?   246,425 or 280,081

8. Which is smaller?   315,417 or 384,672

9. Which is larger?   872,148 or 806,621

13. Which is smaller?   560,060 or 543,385

14. Which is smaller?   739,229 or 754,328

16. Which is larger?   220,144 or 259,877

17. Which is smaller?   787,391 or 714,667

18. Which is smaller?   109,217 or 137,460

Down

1. Which is smaller?   514,853 or 567,285

2. Which is smaller?   988,255 or 905,578

3. Which is larger?   662,484 or 606,103

4. Which is larger?   442,145 or 491,803

5. Which is smaller?   738,633 or 703,406

8. Which is smaller?   356,232 or 319,736

10. Which is smaller?   740,809 or 719,235

11. Which is smaller?   141,754 or 133,068

12. Which is larger?   681,999 or 636,520

15. Which is smaller?   957,052 or 928,489

Puzzle 5   ƍ ◉ ƍ ◉ ƍ ◉ ƍ ƍ ƍ ◉ ◉ ◉ ƍ ◉ ƍ

Can You Find It?

Read each clue. Write the number from the Number Bank that matches the clue in the number puzzle on page 9.

Across

3. 1 in the ten thousands place: _____

5. 8 in the thousands place: _____

6. 6 in the hundred thousands place: _____

7. 4 in the hundred thousands place: _____

12. 5 in the millions place: _____

14. The smaller number that has a 3 in the millions

place: _____

16. 0 in the ten thousands place: _____

17. 9 in the millions place: _____

19. 2 in the tens place: _____

Down

1. 7 in the thousands place: _____

2. 3 in the ones place: _____

4. 4 in the ten thousands place: _____

7. 6 in the ones place: _____

8. The smaller number that has a 9 in the hundred thousands

place: _____

9. 1 in the hundreds place: _____

10. 0 in the ones place: _____

11. 7 in the millions place: _____

13. The larger number that has a 5 in the ten thousands

place: _____

15. 2 in the ones place: _____

18. 8 in the millions place: _____

Number Bank

1,098,867

1,653,457

1,863,161

2,426,341

2,500,011

2,735,240

2,830,456

2,933,847

3,090,665

3,376,829

4,229,762

4,249,285

4,997,984

5,575,065

6,514,694

6,852,019

6,861,533

7,391,837

8,789,938

9,722,491

Puzzle 5

Can You Find It? *(cont.)*

See page 8 for the Across and Down clues.

Puzzle 6

All in Order!

Rewrite the numbers from the Number Bank on the lines in numerical order from least to greatest. Then, using the Across and Down clues, find the number from your new list that the clues are describing and write that number in the number puzzle on page 11. See #2 Across. It has been done for you.

Number Bank
6,646,360
2,561,316
3,899,056
8,732,457
4,115,452
~~2,803,359~~
7,128,470
1,823,419
8,156,820
4,645,213
5,295,164
7,613,871
9,969,097
3,387,569
2,441,368
3,719,002
2,470,545
5,728,249
8,938,899
7,716,070

1. _____
2. _____
3. _____
4. _____
5. ___2,803,359___
6. _____
7. _____
8. _____
9. _____
10. _____
11. _____
12. _____
13. _____
14. _____
15. _____
16. _____
17. _____
18. _____
19. _____
20. _____

Across

2. 5th number
7. 18th number
8. 1st number
10. 12th number
12. 14th number
13. 13th number
14. 4th number
17. 17th number
18. 19th number
19. 16th number
20. 9th number

Down

1. 20th number
3. 6th number
4. 10th number
5. 7th number
6. 15th number
9. 3rd number
11. 2nd number
15. 11th number
16. 8th number

Puzzle 6

All in Order! *(cont.)*

See page 10 for the Across and Down clues.

5 54 10 18 26

2	8	0	3	3	5	9

Puzzle 7

Name That Shape!

Look at the shapes shown below as clues. Find the name of each shape in the Word Bank and write it on the correct line below. Then, rewrite all the shape names in their correct spots in the number puzzle on page 13.

Word Bank

circle	hexagon	pyramid	sphere
cone	octagon	rectangle	square
cube	parallelogram	rectangular prism	trapezoid
cylinder	pentagon	rhombus	triangle

Across

4. _____

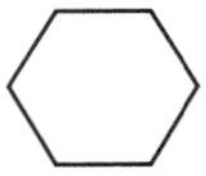

5. _____

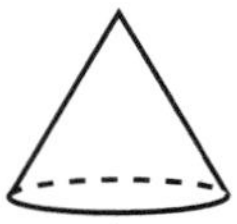

6. _____

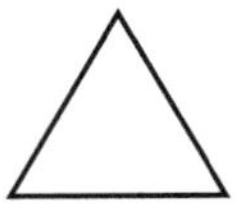

8. _____

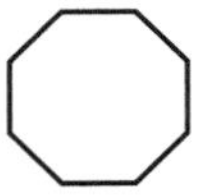

9. _____

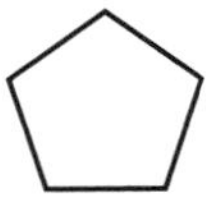

12. _____

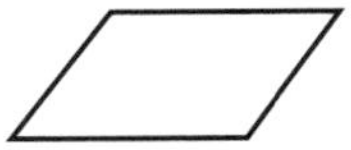

13. _____

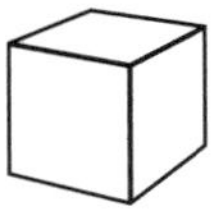

14. _____

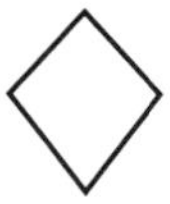

15. _____

Down

1. _____

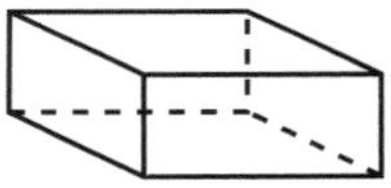

2. _____

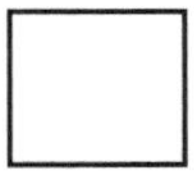

3. _____

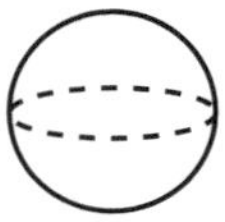

5. _____

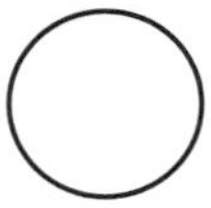

7. _____

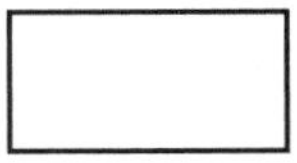

10. _____

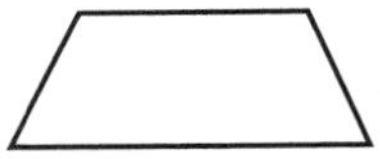

11. _____

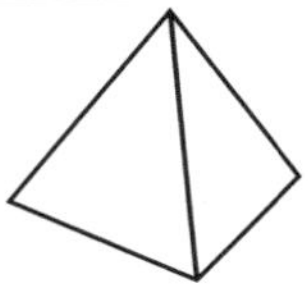

Puzzle 7

Name That Shape! *(cont.)*

See page 12 for the Across and Down clues.

Puzzle 8

Time for Trivia

Answer each trivia question in the box below. Then, use your answers to solve the math problems in each clue. Write these answers in the number puzzle on page 15.

Name the number of. . .

1. pips on a die: _____
2. days in a week: _____
3. months in a year: _____
4. days in a year: _____
5. items in a dozen: _____
6. minutes in an hour: _____
7. hours in a day: _____
8. years in a decade: _____
9. pennies in a dollar: _____
10. states in the U.S.A.: _____
11. fingers and toes on a person: _____
12. seasons in a year: _____
13. sheets in a ream of paper: _____
14. weeks in a year: _____
15. buttons on a push button phone: _____
16. letters in the alphabet: _____
17. items in a gross: _____
18. pounds in a ton: _____
19. things in a pair: _____
20. sides on a pentagon: _____

Across

1. The number of minutes in an hour + the number of weeks in a year = _____
3. The number of buttons on a push button phone x the number in a dozen = _____
4. The number of days in a year ÷ the number of sides on a pentagon = _____
6. The number of letters in the alphabet + the number of weeks in a year = _____
8. The number of fingers and toes + the number of letters in the alphabet = _____
10. The number of pips on a die x the number of minutes in an hour = _____
12. The number of sheets in a ream of paper – the number of pennies in a dollar = _____
13. The number of sides on a pentagon x the number of items in a gross = _____
14. The number of pounds in a ton ÷ the number of years in a decade = _____
15. The number of hours in a day x the number of things in a pair = _____

Down

1. The number of pips on a die x the number of days in a week = _____
2. The number of pennies in a dollar ÷ the number of seasons in a year = _____
3. The number of pounds in a ton – the number of items in a gross = _____
5. The number of days in a year – the number of hours in a day = _____
7. The number of days in a week x the number of months in a year = _____
9. The number of states in the U.S.A. x the number of buttons on a push button phone = _____
11. The number of sheets in a ream of paper ÷ the number of things in a pair = _____
12. The number of years in a decade x the number of seasons in a year = _____
13. The number of pennies in a dollar – the number of fingers and toes – the number of things in a pair = _____
14. The number of months in a year + the number of items in a dozen = _____

Puzzle 8

Time for Trivia *(cont.)*

See page 14 for the Across and Down clues.

Puzzle 9

Let's Get Adding!

Solve each addition problem. Write each sum in the number puzzle.

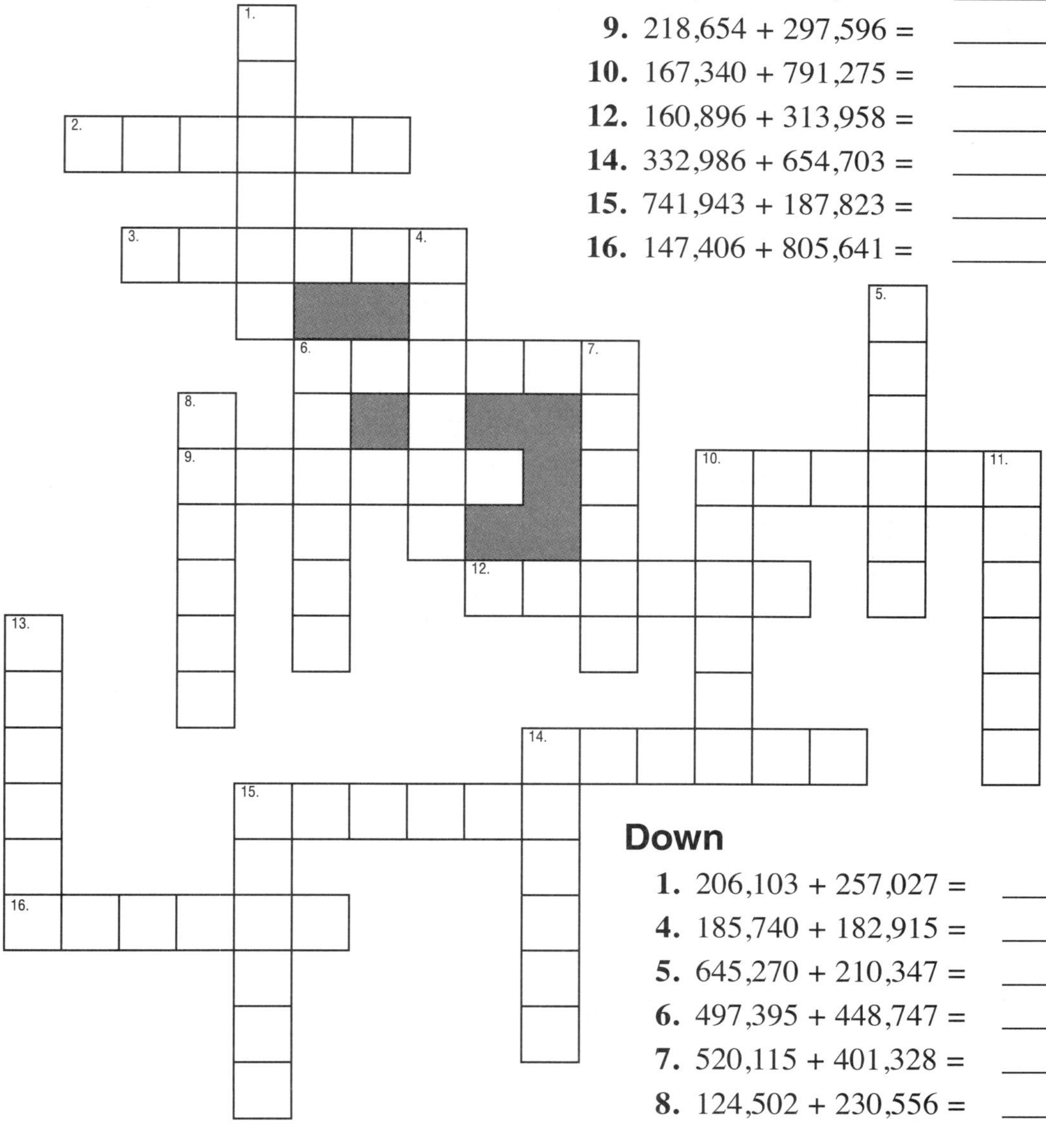

Across

2. $133,455 + 287,869 =$ _____

3. $299,547 + 433,846 =$ _____

6. $277,490 + 661,379 =$ _____

9. $218,654 + 297,596 =$ _____

10. $167,340 + 791,275 =$ _____

12. $160,896 + 313,958 =$ _____

14. $332,986 + 654,703 =$ _____

15. $741,943 + 187,823 =$ _____

16. $147,406 + 805,641 =$ _____

Down

1. $206,103 + 257,027 =$ _____

4. $185,740 + 182,915 =$ _____

5. $645,270 + 210,347 =$ _____

6. $497,395 + 448,747 =$ _____

7. $520,115 + 401,328 =$ _____

8. $124,502 + 230,556 =$ _____

10. $288,905 + 636,631 =$ _____

11. $199,116 + 344,863 =$ _____

13. $290,756 + 155,003 =$ _____

14. $382,796 + 586,428 =$ _____

15. $162,829 + 811,867 =$ _____

Puzzle 10

Adding to the Hundred Thousands

Solve each addition problem. Write each sum in the number puzzle.

Across

2. 801,633 + 124,091 = _____

6. 734,296 + 233,823 = _____

8. 108,768 + 159,265 = _____

9. 458,202 + 147,752 = _____

12. 608,931 + 234,374 = _____

13. 705,966 + 215,729 = _____

14. 617,429 + 361,410 = _____

16. 556,302 + 198,261 = _____

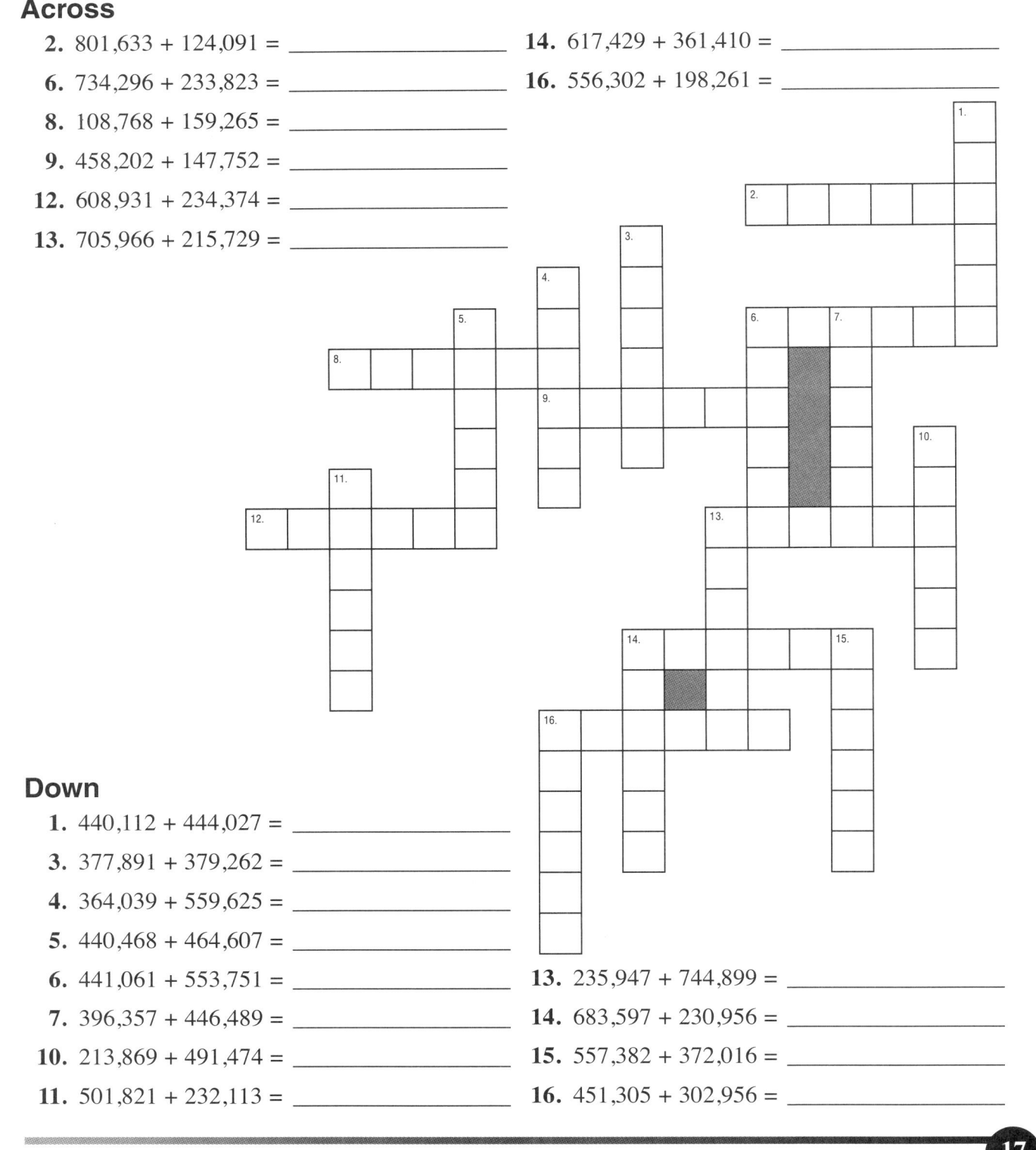

Down

1. 440,112 + 444,027 = _____

3. 377,891 + 379,262 = _____

4. 364,039 + 559,625 = _____

5. 440,468 + 464,607 = _____

6. 441,061 + 553,751 = _____

7. 396,357 + 446,489 = _____

10. 213,869 + 491,474 = _____

11. 501,821 + 232,113 = _____

13. 235,947 + 744,899 = _____

14. 683,597 + 230,956 = _____

15. 557,382 + 372,016 = _____

16. 451,305 + 302,956 = _____

Puzzle 11

You Do the Math!

Solve each subtraction problem. Write each difference in the number puzzle.

Across

3. 420,638 – 326,663 = _____

5. 897,382 – 818,265 = _____

9. 321,371 – 136,972 = _____

12. 960,595 – 659,745 = _____

13. 865,927 – 754,611 = _____

15. 701,129 – 494,397 = _____

17. 628,493 – 560,448 = _____

18. 718,700 – 411,099 = _____

19. 434,075 – 250,997 = _____

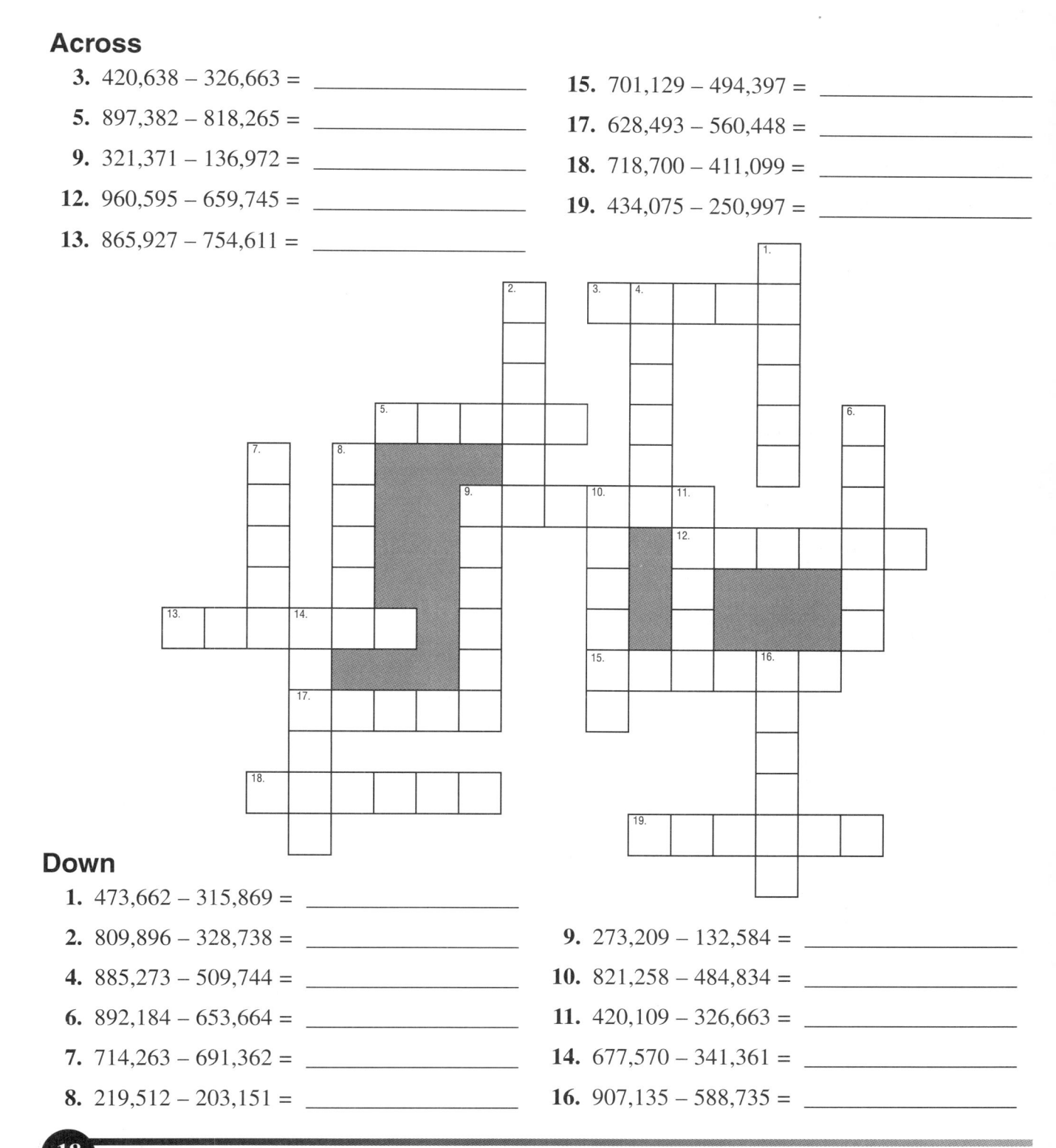

Down

1. 473,662 – 315,869 = _____

2. 809,896 – 328,738 = _____

4. 885,273 – 509,744 = _____

6. 892,184 – 653,664 = _____

7. 714,263 – 691,362 = _____

8. 219,512 – 203,151 = _____

9. 273,209 – 132,584 = _____

10. 821,258 – 484,834 = _____

11. 420,109 – 326,663 = _____

14. 677,570 – 341,361 = _____

16. 907,135 – 588,735 = _____

Puzzle 12

More Subtraction Practice

Solve each subtraction problem. Write each difference in the number puzzle.

Across

1. 676,769 – 381,079 = _____

3. 898,431 – 547,265 = _____

5. 281,241 – 139,345 = _____

6. 9,198,177 – 5,709,765 = _____

10. 607,769 – 381,079 = _____

11. 849,009 – 381,354 = _____

14. 8,053,459 – 3,879,032 = _____

15. 327,677 – 248,198 = _____

17. 856,376 – 551,320 = _____

18. 8,548,776 – 4,160,198 = _____

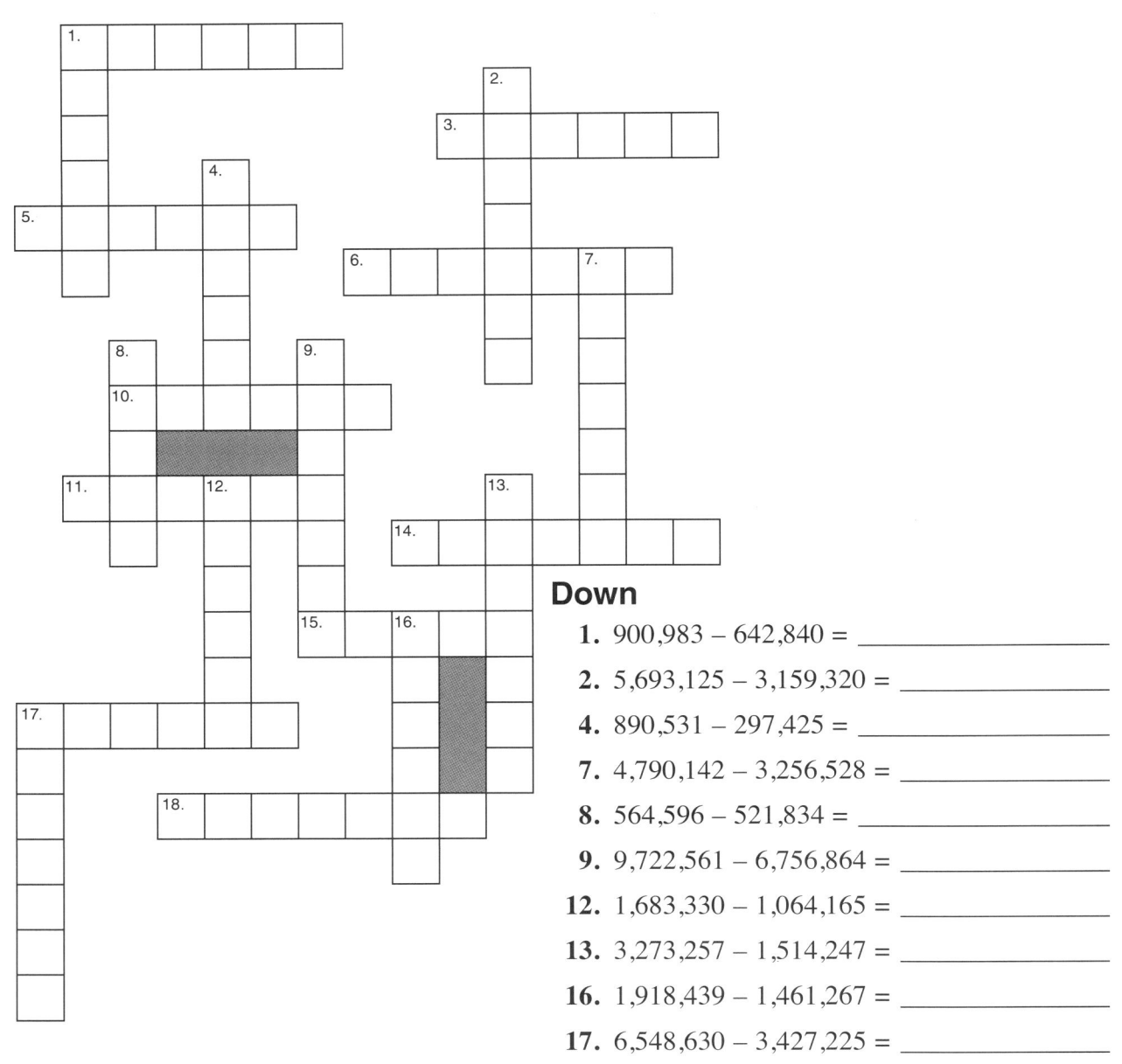

Down

1. 900,983 – 642,840 = _____

2. 5,693,125 – 3,159,320 = _____

4. 890,531 – 297,425 = _____

7. 4,790,142 – 3,256,528 = _____

8. 564,596 – 521,834 = _____

9. 9,722,561 – 6,756,864 = _____

12. 1,683,330 – 1,064,165 = _____

13. 3,273,257 – 1,514,247 = _____

16. 1,918,439 – 1,461,267 = _____

17. 6,548,630 – 3,427,225 = _____

#3909 Practice Makes Perfect: Number Puzzles

Puzzle 13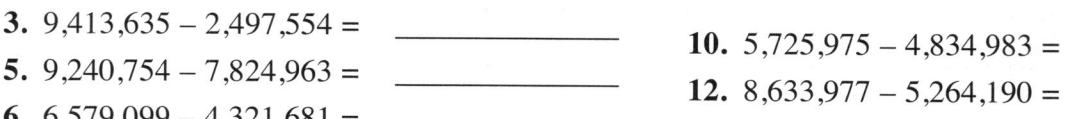

Subtraction in the Millions

Solve each subtraction problem. Write each difference in the number puzzle.

Across

3. 9,413,635 − 2,497,554 = _____

5. 9,240,754 − 7,824,963 = _____

6. 6,579,099 − 4,321,681 = _____

8. 6,046,251 − 5,910,806 = _____

9. 9,307,641 − 3,921,217 = _____

10. 5,725,975 − 4,834,983 = _____

12. 8,633,977 − 5,264,190 = _____

16. 6,198,739 − 5,036,259 = _____

17. 1,768,954 − 1,733,569 = _____

18. 8,833,551 − 7,586,983 = _____

Down

1. 4,137,122 − 3,425,497 = _____

2. 7,695,400 − 7,079,668 = _____

4. 8,497,729 − 6,611,811 = _____

7. 7,228,739 − 2,964,461 = _____

8. 8,343,206 − 7,012,063 = _____

11. 8,307,656 − 5,820,178 = _____

12. 7,120,782 − 4,005,685 = _____

13. 2,135,881 − 1,843,313 = _____

14. 9,441,563 − 6,258,202 = _____

15. 4,132,095 − 2,442,989 = _____

Puzzle 14

Extra Practice with Adding and Subtracting

Solve each problem. Write each answer in the number puzzle.

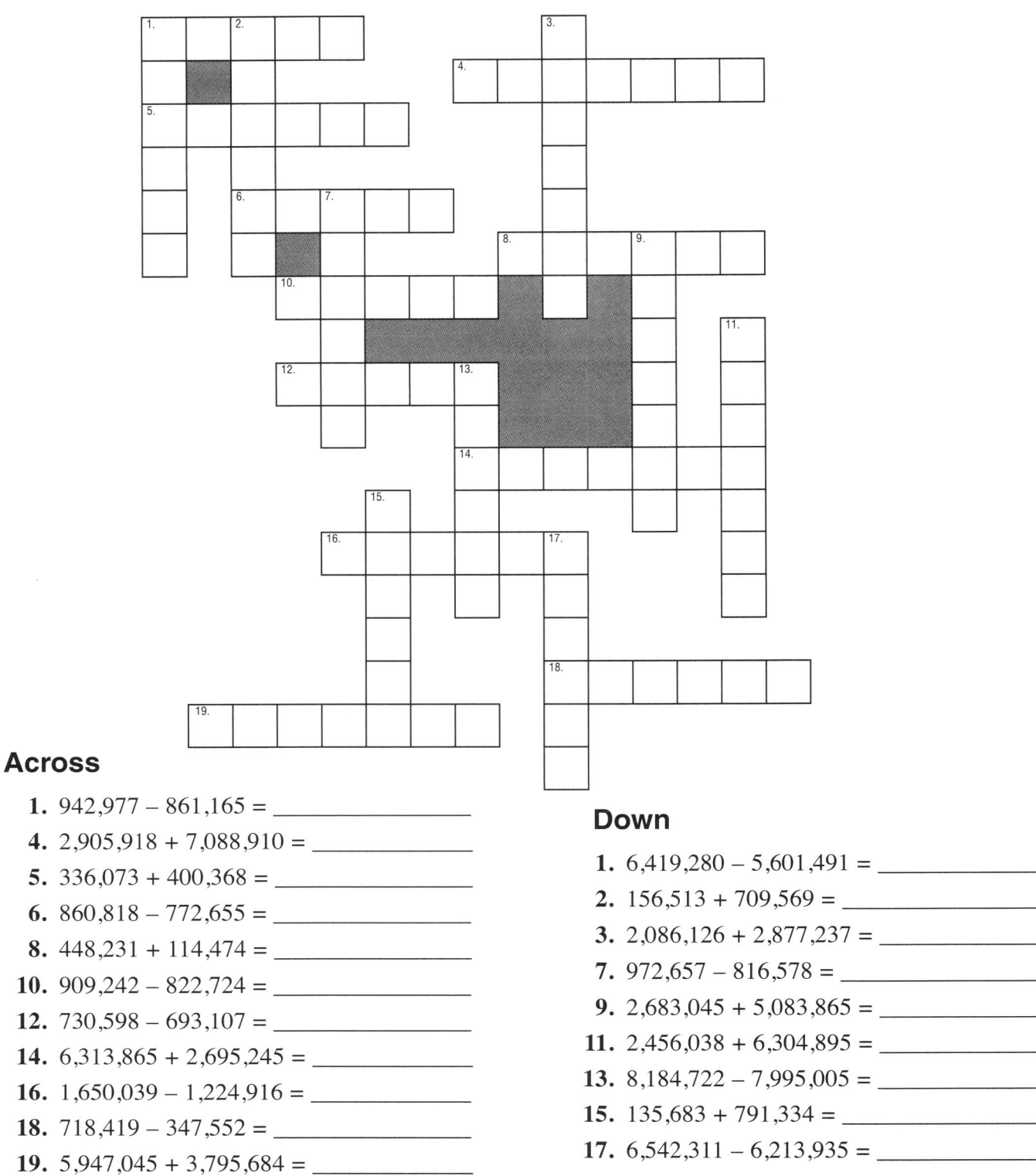

Across

1. 942,977 − 861,165 = _____

4. 2,905,918 + 7,088,910 = _____

5. 336,073 + 400,368 = _____

6. 860,818 − 772,655 = _____

8. 448,231 + 114,474 = _____

10. 909,242 − 822,724 = _____

12. 730,598 − 693,107 = _____

14. 6,313,865 + 2,695,245 = _____

16. 1,650,039 − 1,224,916 = _____

18. 718,419 − 347,552 = _____

19. 5,947,045 + 3,795,684 = _____

Down

1. 6,419,280 − 5,601,491 = _____

2. 156,513 + 709,569 = _____

3. 2,086,126 + 2,877,237 = _____

7. 972,657 − 816,578 = _____

9. 2,683,045 + 5,083,865 = _____

11. 2,456,038 + 6,304,895 = _____

13. 8,184,722 − 7,995,005 = _____

15. 135,683 + 791,334 = _____

17. 6,542,311 − 6,213,935 = _____

Puzzle 15

What's Missing?

Complete each number sentence by writing in the missing factors on the lines below that would make both sides equal. Write each answer as a **number word** in the number puzzle. See #1 Across. It has been done for you.

Across

1. 25 x 2 = 10 x _____5_____

2. 6 x 2 = _____ x 4

4. 3 x 14 = _____ x 6

5. 4 x 13 = 52 x _____

8. 4 x 20 = _____ x 5

9. 8 x 5 = 4 x _____

11. 22 x 2 = 1 x _____

13. 15 x 4 = 3 x _____

15. 3 x 8 = _____ x 6

17. 1 x 39 = 3 x _____

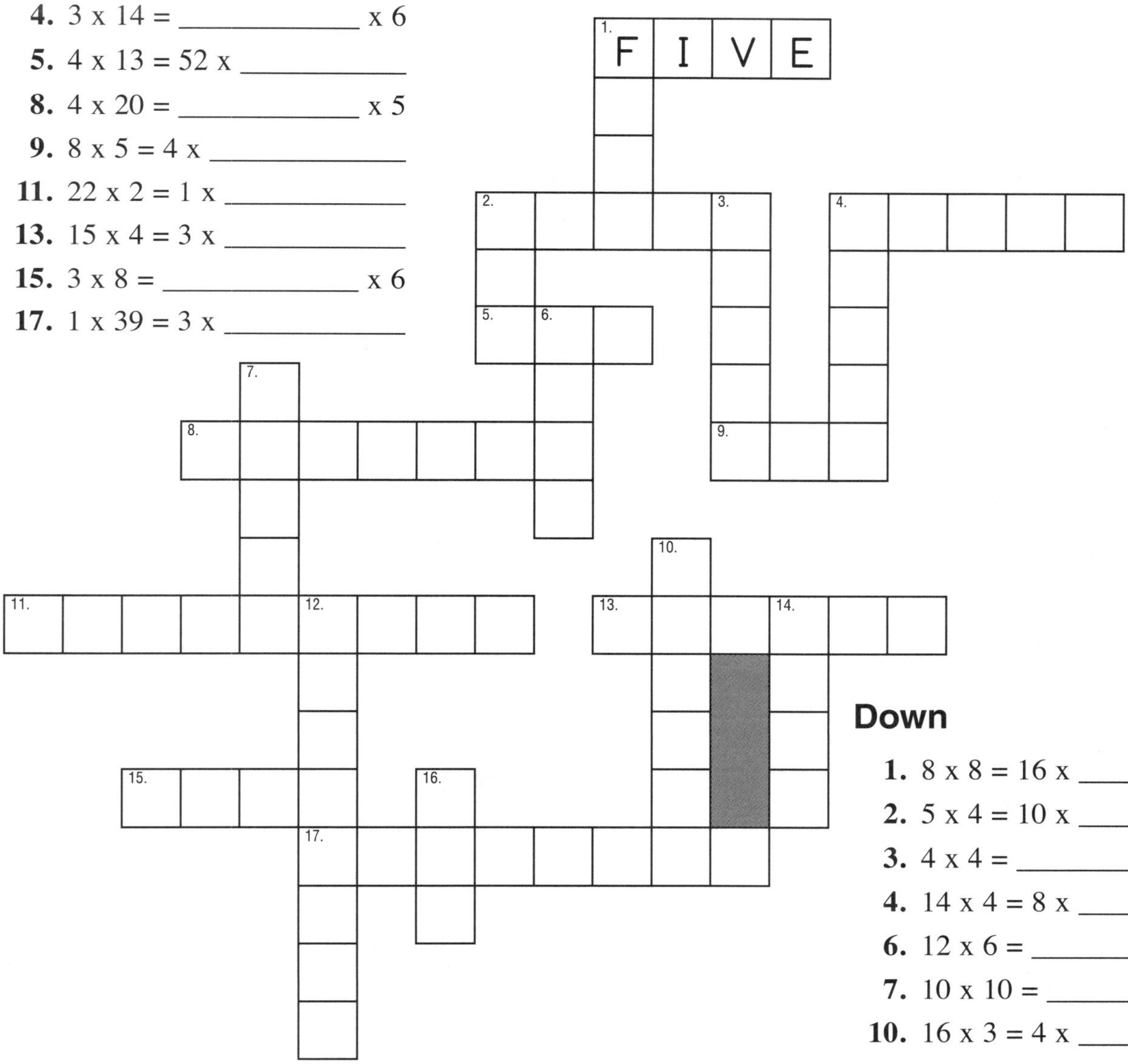

Down

1. 8 x 8 = 16 x _____

2. 5 x 4 = 10 x _____

3. 4 x 4 = _____ x 2

4. 14 x 4 = 8 x _____

6. 12 x 6 = _____ x 8

7. 10 x 10 = _____ x 2

10. 16 x 3 = 4 x _____

12. 28 x 2 = _____ x 4

14. 6 x 6 = 4 x _____

16. 10 x 3 = 5 x _____

1. F I V E

Puzzle 16

Multiplying by One Digit

Solve each multiplication problem. Write each product in the number puzzle.

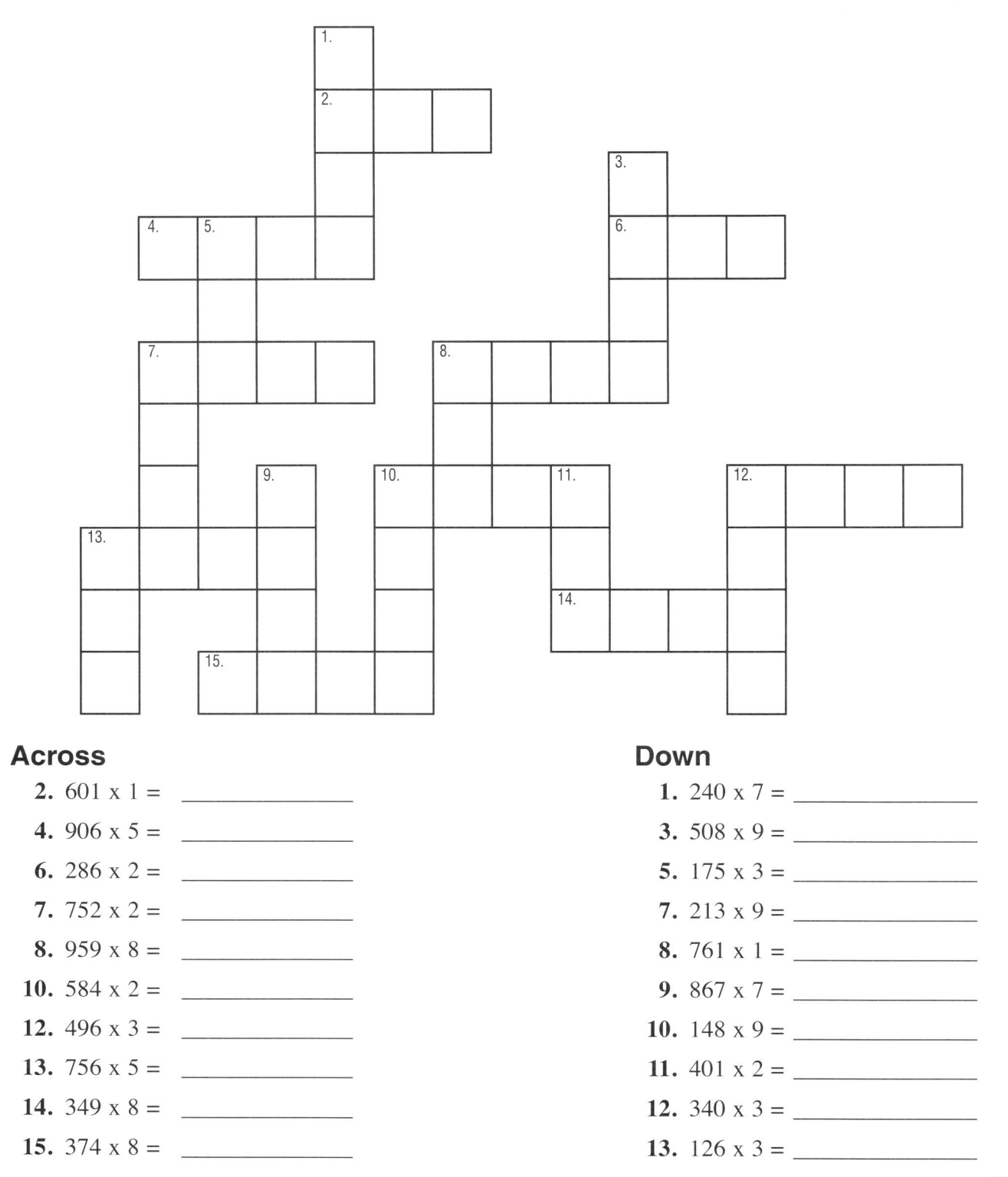

Across

2. 601 x 1 = _____

4. 906 x 5 = _____

6. 286 x 2 = _____

7. 752 x 2 = _____

8. 959 x 8 = _____

10. 584 x 2 = _____

12. 496 x 3 = _____

13. 756 x 5 = _____

14. 349 x 8 = _____

15. 374 x 8 = _____

Down

1. 240 x 7 = _____

3. 508 x 9 = _____

5. 175 x 3 = _____

7. 213 x 9 = _____

8. 761 x 1 = _____

9. 867 x 7 = _____

10. 148 x 9 = _____

11. 401 x 2 = _____

12. 340 x 3 = _____

13. 126 x 3 = _____

Puzzle 17

Multiplying Multiple Digits

Solve each multiplication problem. Write each product in the number puzzle.

Across

1. 7,648 x 4 = _____

2. 7,486 x 6 = _____

3. 9,755 x 4 = _____

5. 2,748 x 3 = _____

7. 2,065 x 3 = _____

11. 3,796 x 2 = _____

12. 9,530 x 2 = _____

13. 1,402 x 1 = _____

15. 8,376 x 2 = _____

16. 9,907 x 4 = _____

17. 7,962 x 3 = _____

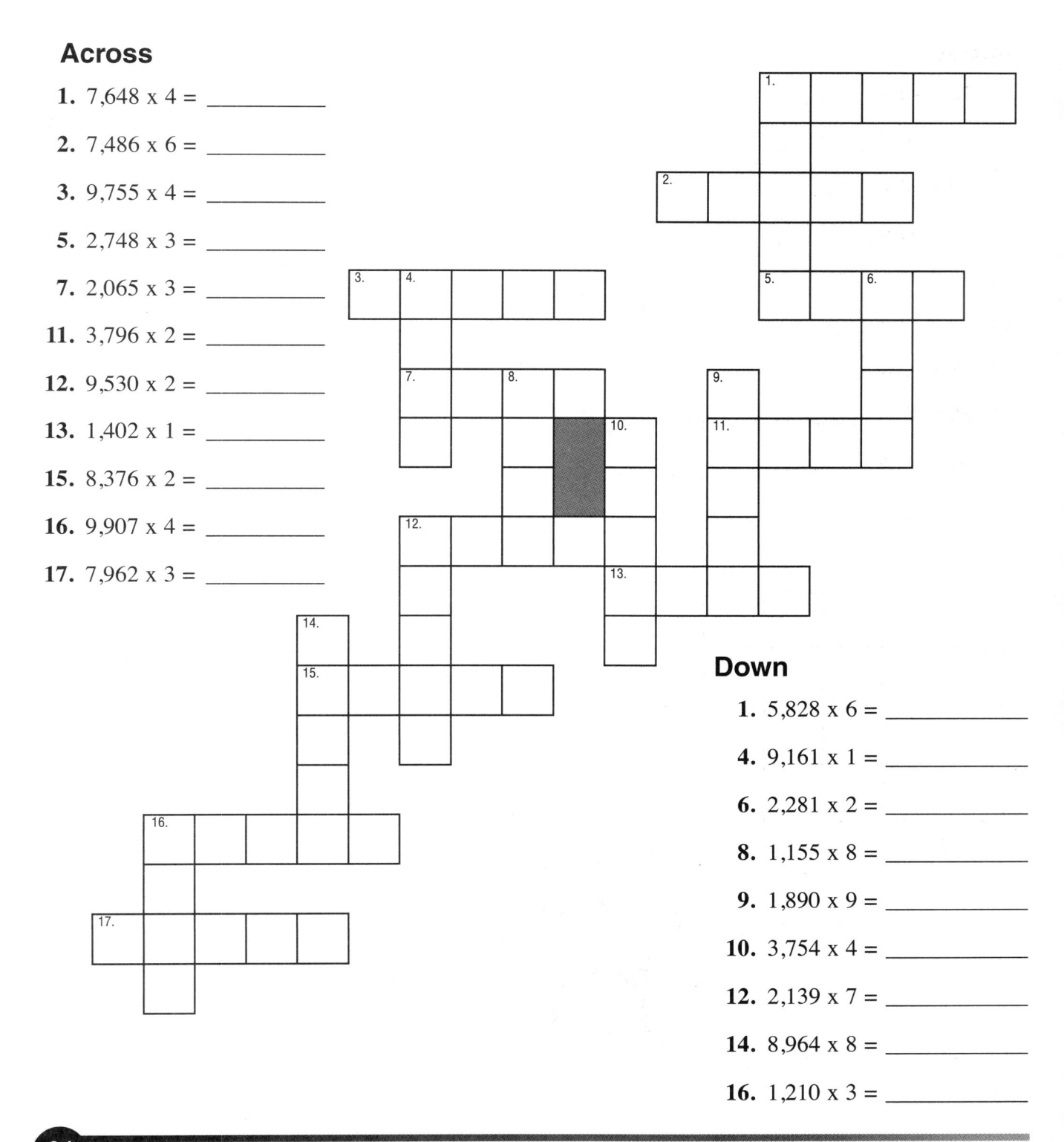

Down

1. 5,828 x 6 = _____

4. 9,161 x 1 = _____

6. 2,281 x 2 = _____

8. 1,155 x 8 = _____

9. 1,890 x 9 = _____

10. 3,754 x 4 = _____

12. 2,139 x 7 = _____

14. 8,964 x 8 = _____

16. 1,210 x 3 = _____

Puzzle 18

Multiplication by Tens

Solve each multiplication problem. Write each product in the number puzzle.

Across

2. 20 x 90 = _____

3. 38 x 40 = _____

7. 56 x 50 = _____

8. 17 x 60 = _____

10. 10 x 79 = _____

12. 47 x 50 = _____

13. 18 x 50 = _____

16. 30 x 80 = _____

17. 64 x 80 = _____

Down

1. 60 x 85 = _____

3. 10 x 12 = _____

4. 28 x 80 = _____

5. 90 x 87 = _____

6. 73 x 10 = _____

8. 70 x 19 = _____

9. 60 x 40 = _____

11. 10 x 92 = _____

13. 10 x 96 = _____

14. 29 x 50 = _____

15. 75 x 30 = _____

Puzzle 19

Multiplying by 10, 11, 12, and 13

Solve each multiplication problem. Write each product in the number puzzle.

Across

1. 684 x 10 = _____

3. 475 x 11 = _____

5. 102 x 13 = _____

7. 197 x 11 = _____

10. 370 x 13 = _____

11. 295 x 10 = _____

12. 308 x 13 = _____

13. 139 x 12 = _____

15. 620 x 13 = _____

17. 745 x 12 = _____

19. 253 x 11 = _____

Down

2. 796 x 11 = _____

4. 518 x 11 = _____

6. 281 x 12 = _____

8. 177 x 10 = _____

9. 122 x 13 = _____

12. 342 x 12 = _____

14. 693 x 10 = _____

16. 263 x 11 = _____

18. 446 x 10 = _____

Puzzle 20

Multiplication Challenge

Solve each multiplication problem. Write each product in the number puzzle.

Across

2. 1,915 x 66 = _____

3. 6,028 x 32 = _____

6. 8,811 x 56 = _____

7. 4,397 x 20 = _____

9. 6,449 x 96 = _____

13. 7,073 x 77 = _____

16. 1,628 x 36 = _____

17. 8,244 x 35 = _____

18. 6,864 x 64 = _____

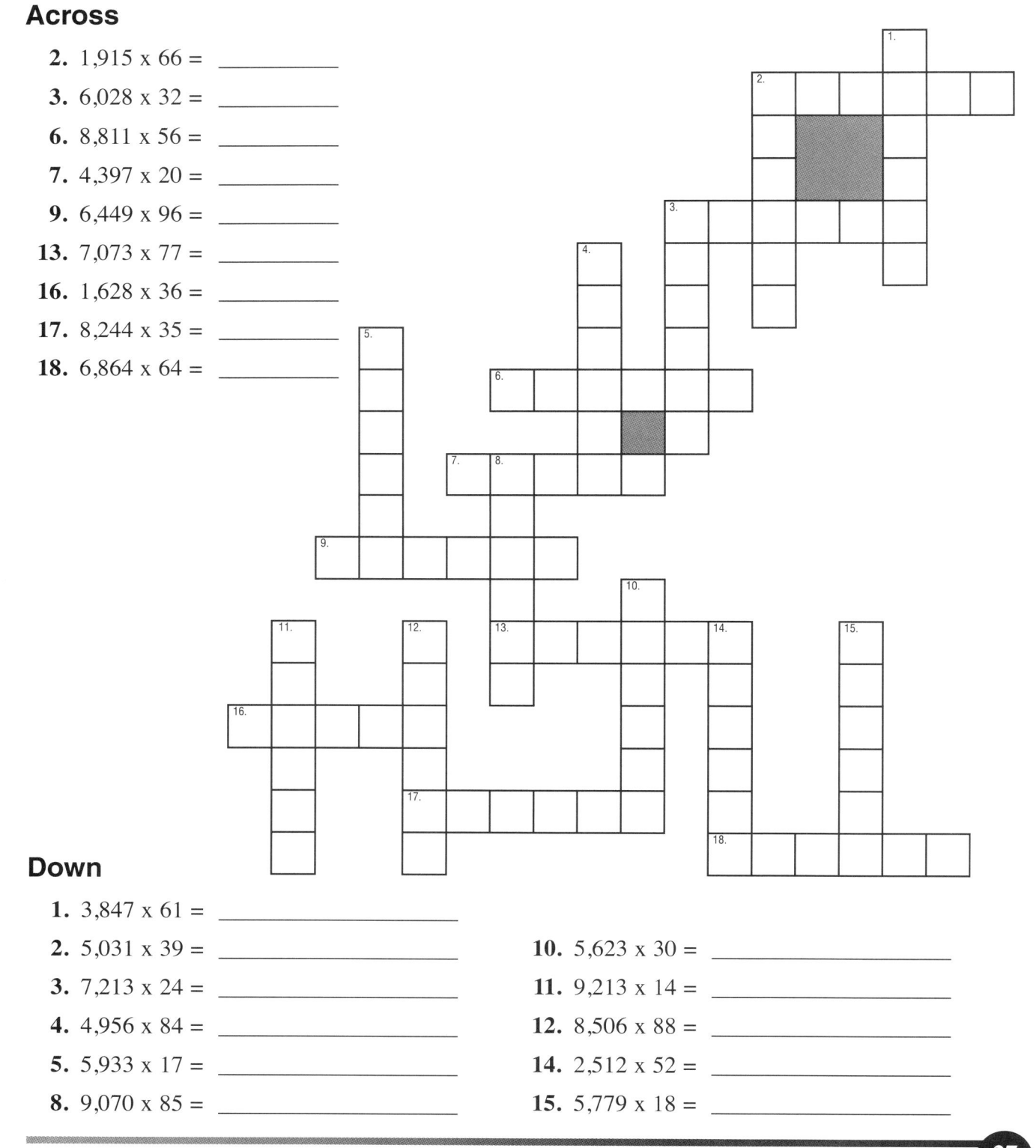

Down

1. 3,847 x 61 = _____

2. 5,031 x 39 = _____

3. 7,213 x 24 = _____

4. 4,956 x 84 = _____

5. 5,933 x 17 = _____

8. 9,070 x 85 = _____

10. 5,623 x 30 = _____

11. 9,213 x 14 = _____

12. 8,506 x 88 = _____

14. 2,512 x 52 = _____

15. 5,779 x 18 = _____

Puzzle 21

Prime Time

Look at each pair of numbers below. Circle the one that is a prime number. Write each prime number in the number puzzle.

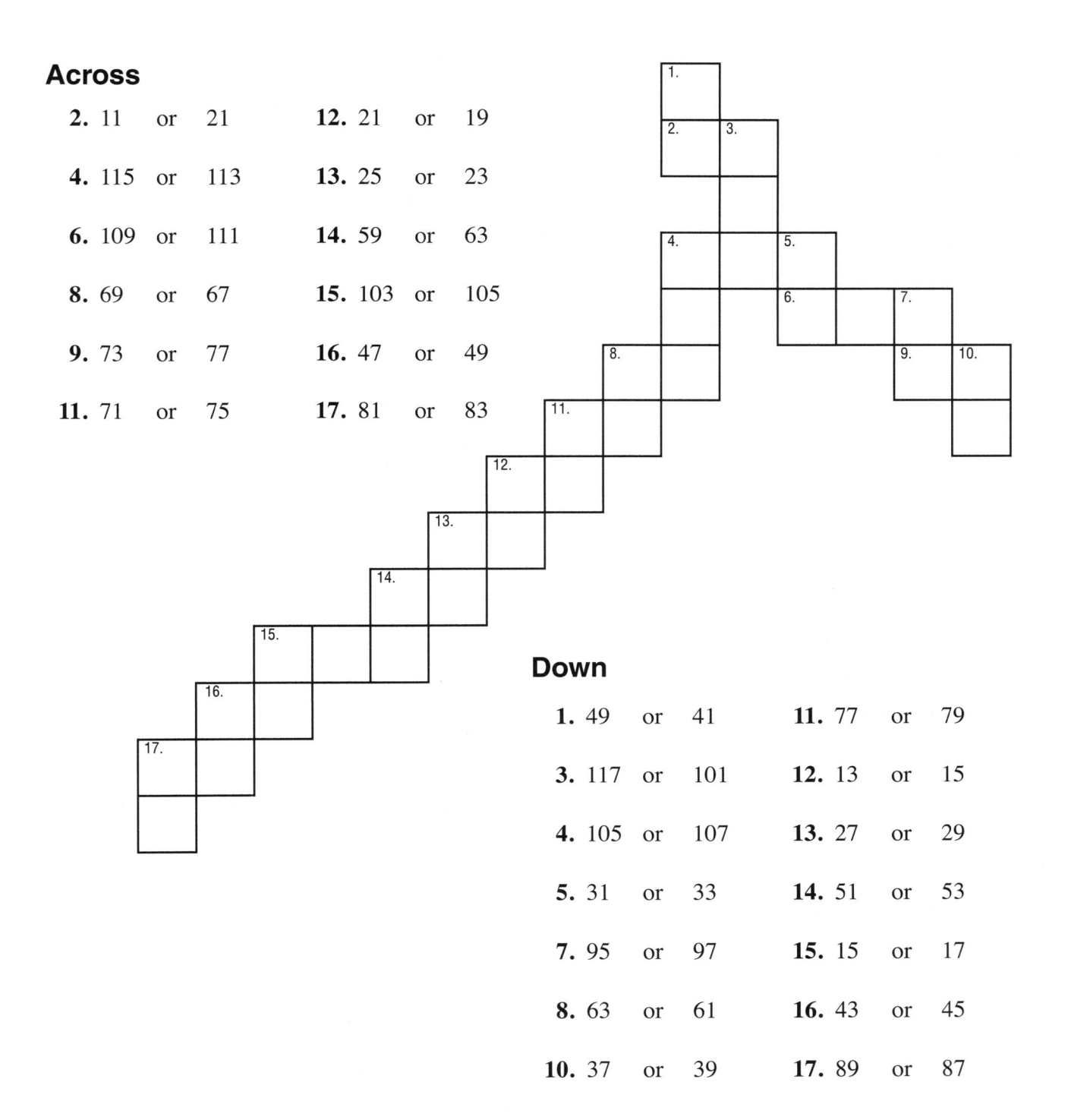

Across

2. 11 or 21

4. 115 or 113

6. 109 or 111

8. 69 or 67

9. 73 or 77

11. 71 or 75

12. 21 or 19

13. 25 or 23

14. 59 or 63

15. 103 or 105

16. 47 or 49

17. 81 or 83

Down

1. 49 or 41

3. 117 or 101

4. 105 or 107

5. 31 or 33

7. 95 or 97

8. 63 or 61

10. 37 or 39

11. 77 or 79

12. 13 or 15

13. 27 or 29

14. 51 or 53

15. 15 or 17

16. 43 or 45

17. 89 or 87

Puzzle 22 ౨ ❂ ౨ ❂ ౨ ❂ ౨ ❂ ౨ ౨ ౨ ❂ ౨ ❂

Division Practice

Solve each division problem. Write each quotient in the number puzzle.

Across

1. 968 ÷ 8 = _____

3. 2,928 ÷ 4 = _____

5. 845 ÷ 5 = _____

6. 275 ÷ 5 = _____

7. 4,164 ÷ 6 = _____

8. 166 ÷ 2 = _____

9. 114 ÷ 6 = _____

10. 813 ÷ 3 = _____

11. 980 ÷ 10 = _____

12. 8,631 ÷ 7 = _____

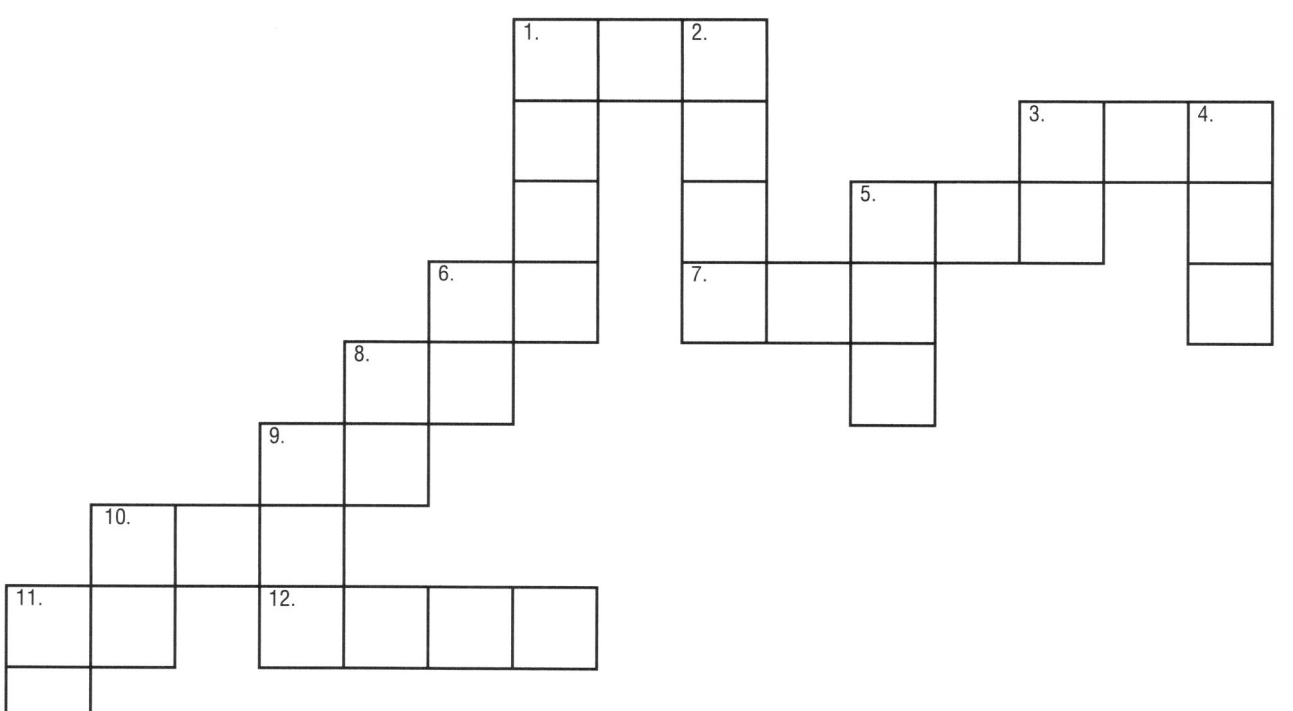

Down

1. 9,765 ÷ 9 = _____

2. 5,238 ÷ 3 = _____

3. 237 ÷ 3 = _____

4. 514 ÷ 2 = _____

5. 876 ÷ 6 = _____

6. 477 ÷ 9 = _____

8. 534 ÷ 6 = _____

9. 777 ÷ 7 = _____

10. 196 ÷ 7 = _____

11. 485 ÷ 5 = _____

Puzzle 23 ✺ ✺ ✺ ✺ ✺ ✺ ✺ ✺ ✺ ✺ ✺ ✺ ✺

Division of Five-Digit Numbers

Solve each division problem. Write each quotient in the number puzzle.

Across

1. $53{,}690 \div 10 =$ _____

3. $75{,}834 \div 6 =$ _____

7. $73{,}745 \div 5 =$ _____

8. $80{,}397 \div 9 =$ _____

9. $50{,}548 \div 4 =$ _____

11. $63{,}056 \div 8 =$ _____

12. $54{,}064 \div 8 =$ _____

13. $58{,}372 \div 2 =$ _____

16. $36{,}153 \div 9 =$ _____

17. $53{,}669 \div 7 =$ _____

18. $21{,}837 \div 3 =$ _____

Down

2. $12{,}098 \div 2 =$ _____

4. $68{,}349 \div 3 =$ _____

5. $72{,}681 \div 7 =$ _____

6. $22{,}185 \div 5 =$ _____

9. $38{,}013 \div 3 =$ _____

10. $29{,}420 \div 4 =$ _____

14. $89{,}110 \div 10 =$ _____

15. $44{,}178 \div 6 =$ _____

16. $42{,}993 \div 9 =$ _____

Puzzle 24 ꙮ ꙮ ꙮ ꙮ ꙮ ꙮ ꙮ ꙮ ꙮ ꙮ ꙮ ꙮ ꙮ ꙮ

The Event

Write each number in standard form directly onto the number puzzle on page 32.

Across

3. Clint used six million, twenty-three thousand, four hundred eighty-three roses on the float.
5. Dina counted three million, two hundred ninety-three thousand, six hundred four people at the event.
7. Jeff saw two million, five hundred ninety-seven thousand, three hundred fifty-three people on the sidewalk.
9. Terri sold nine million, six hundred eighty-four thousand, six hundred ninety-seven commemorative programs.
12. Marty developed one million, seven hundred two thousand, three hundred fifty rolls of film.
15. Edie sold six million, one hundred twenty-four thousand, six hundred seventy-nine patriotic hats.
17. Mark made six million, five hundred seventy-two thousand, eight hundred ninety-eight hot dogs.
18. Eva popped four million, six hundred eighty-one thousand, five hundred thirteen kernels of popcorn.
19. The news media wrote five million, forty-seven thousand, seven hundred one words about the event.
20. Nine million, two hundred twenty-seven thousand, two hundred eighty-six people watched the event on television.

Down

1. Eight million, seven hundred fifty-six thousand, one hundred seventy-eight pounds of trash were picked up the next day.
2. Two million, two hundred sixty-two thousand, nine hundred sixty-seven people listened to the event on the radio.
4. Four million, seven hundred forty-five thousand, nine hundred forty-nine shirts were sold.
6. Nine million, six hundred seventy thousand, fifty-one people watched the event from around the world.
8. Five million, twelve thousand, four hundred ninety-four dollars were donated to the event.
10. It took six million, two hundred eighty-seven thousand, thirty-one people to decorate for the event.
11. Four million, eight hundred eighty-nine thousand, eight hundred thirty-four people put on their own mini-event parties.
13. Five million, one hundred ninety-eight thousand, five hundred seven people carpooled to the event.
14. The police wrote three million, one hundred eighty-one thousand, five hundred seventy-eight tickets to cars parked in "No Parking" spots.
16. Nine million, six hundred sixteen thousand, five hundred twenty-three people were glad the event was over!

Puzzle 24

The Event *(cont.)*

See page 31 for the Across and Down clues.

Puzzle 25 ⟳ ☙ ⟳ ☙ ⟳ ☙ ⟳ ☙ ⟳ ⟳ ⟳ ☙ ⟳ ☙ ⟳

The Top Ten at the Music Store

Use the chart below to solve each word problem. Write each answer in the number puzzle on page 34.

Number of Music CDs Sold			
Big Band	23,999	Jazz	55,088
Children's Music	41,580	Pop Music	29,572
Classic Rock	17,736	R & B	37,623
Country Music	96,398	Show Tunes	17,355
Golden Oldies	13,798	Soundtracks	16,040

Across

1. What is the total number of Show Tunes and Golden Oldies CDs sold? _____
4. What is the difference between the number of Jazz CDs and Pop CDs sold? _____
5. What is the difference between the number of R & B CDs and Classic Rock CDs sold? _____
6. What is the difference between the number of Big Band CDs and Soundtracks CDs sold? _____
8. What is the difference between the number of Country Music CDs and Jazz CDs sold? _____
11. What is the difference between the number of Country Music CDs and R & B CDs sold? _____
13. What is the total number of Big Band and Pop Music CDs sold? _____
15. What is the total number of Golden Oldies and Country Music CDs sold? _____
17. What is the total number of Soundtracks and Children's Music CDs sold? _____

Down

2. What is the difference between the number of Classic Rock CDs and Show Tunes CDs sold? _____
3. What is the total number of Classic Rock and Jazz CDs sold? _____
4. What is the difference between the number of Children's Music CDs and Golden Oldies CDs sold? _____
5. What is the difference between the number of Children's Music CDs and Pop Music CDs sold? _____
7. What is the total number of Children's Music and Jazz CDs sold? _____
9. What is the difference between the number of Big Band CDs and Golden Oldies CDs sold? _____
10. What is the difference between the number of Show Tunes CDs and Soundtracks CDs sold? _____
12. What is the total number of Show Tunes and R & B CDs sold? _____
14. What is the total number of Soundtracks and Classic Rock CDs sold? _____
16. What is the total number of Country Music and R & B CDs sold? _____

Puzzle 25

The Top Ten at the Music Store (cont.)

See page 33 for the Across and Down clues.

Puzzle 26

Fireworks for Sale!

Use a calculator to find the total cost (including tax) for each item or items purchased. The tax rate is 6%. Round each answer to the nearest penny. Write each total cost in the number puzzle on page 36. Be sure to include the dollar signs and the decimal points in the puzzle. See #2 Across. It has been done for you.

Fireworks Price List

Firecracker	$2.00	Snail	$1.50
Flame	$4.00	Sparkler	$2.50
Fountain	$8.50	Tornado	$5.50
Pinwheel	$3.00	Twister	$3.50
Rocket	$5.00	Whistler	$4.50

Across	Cost Without Tax	+	Tax	=	Total Cost
2. Jacob buys a sparkler.	$2.50	+	$0.15	=	$2.65
4. Terri buys a snail.		+		=	
5. Christie buys four rockets.		+		=	
7. Angela buys six firecrackers.		+		=	
8. Carole buys a rocket and a tornado.		+		=	
10. Diane buys ten snails.		+		=	
11. Henry buys a rocket.		+		=	
12. Stephen buys a whistler.		+		=	
13. Alyssa buys three firecrackers and two flames.		+		=	

Down	Cost Without Tax	+	Tax	=	Total Cost
1. Maria buys a fountain and a pinwheel.		+		=	
3. Billy buys a tornado.		+		=	
4. Craig buys a tornado and a whistler.		+		=	
5. Vanessa buys a firecracker.		+		=	
6. Marsha buys a twister.		+		=	
7. Pete buys a flame and a fountain.		+		=	
8. George buys three whistlers.		+		=	
9. Marlon buys a whistler and a pinwheel.		+		=	
10. Travis buys a sparkler and two twisters.		+		=	
12. Abe buys a flame.		+		=	

Puzzle 26

Fireworks for Sale! *(cont.)*

See page 35 for the Across and Down clues.

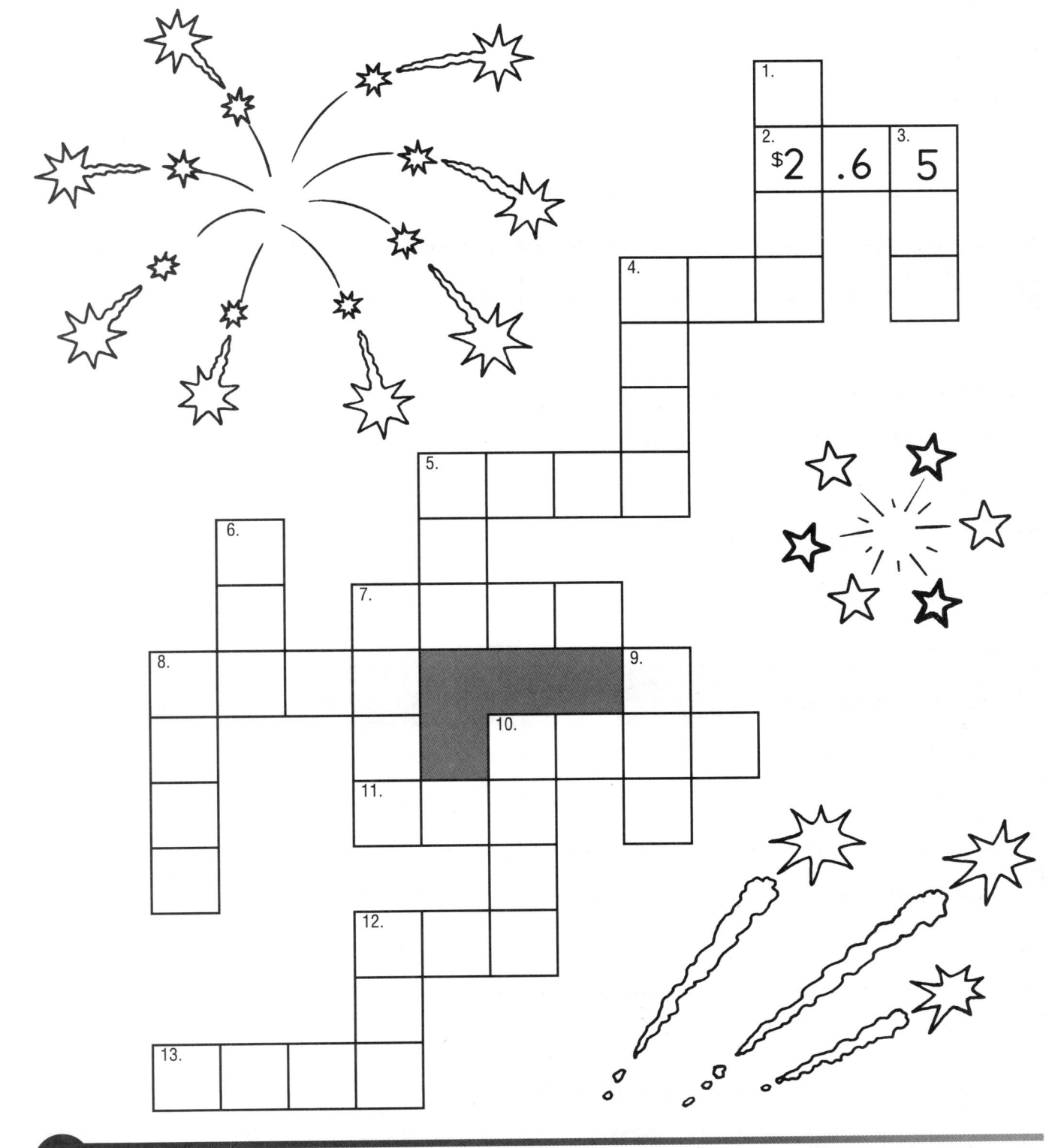

Puzzle 27 ᵔ ᵔ ᵔ ᵔ ᵔ ᵔ ᵔ ᵔ ᵔ ᵔ ᵔ ᵔ ᵔ ᵔ

Can I Get My Change?

Calculate the change needed for each order using the menu on page 38. Write that amount in the number puzzle on page 38. Be sure to include the dollar signs and the decimal points in the puzzle. See #1 Across. It has been done for you.

Across

1. Trista has $6.00. She orders eight orders of fries. How much change is she given? ____$3.44____

3. Betty has $3.00. She orders four orders of fries. How much change is she given?_____

5. Katie has $2.00. She orders a pie. How much change is she given? _____

7. Pete has $7.00. He orders nine cookies. How much change is he given? _____

8. Gayle has $8.00. She orders two kid's meals. How much change is she given?_____

9. Dina has $5.00. She orders four cheeseburgers. How much change is she given? _____

10. Michelle has $4.00. She orders one kid's meal. How much change is she given? _____

12. Inga has $9.00. She orders five salads. How much change is she given? _____

13. Rosa has $8.00. She orders seven salads. How much change is she given? _____

15. Enrique has $6.00. He orders seven cookies. How much change is he given? _____

Down

1. Hank has $8.00. He orders four sodas. How much change is he given? _____

2. Wendy has $6.00. She orders a soda. How much change is she given?_____

3. Van has $2.00. He orders one cheeseburger. How much change is he given?_____

4. Ophelia has $6.00. She orders seven pies. How much change is she given?_____

5. Abel has $2.00. He orders a hamburger. How much change is he given?_____

6. James has $10.00. He orders nine chicken fingers. How much change is he given?_____

7. Luke has $3.00. He orders five milkshakes. How much change is he given? _____

9. Stan has $9.00. He orders nine hamburgers. How much change is he given?_____

11. Norris has $5.00. He orders six chicken fingers. How much change is he given? _____

14. Carlos has $8.00. He orders six milkshakes. How much change is he given?_____

Puzzle 27 ꙮ

Can I Get My Change? *(cont.)*

See page 37 for the Across and Down clues.

Menu

Cheeseburger	$1.00		Hamburger	$0.81
Chicken fingers	$0.74		Milkshake	$0.49
Cookie	$0.72		Pie	$0.57
Kid's Meal	$2.41		Salad	$0.95
Fries	$0.32		Soda	$1.17

Puzzle 28

Money "Cents"

Calculate the total amount of money in each row. Write that amount in the number puzzle on page 40. Be sure to include the dollar signs and the decimal points in the puzzle. See #1 Across. It has been done for you.

Across

	1¢	5¢	10¢	25¢	50¢	$1.00	$5.00	Total
1.	7	1	5	8	4	7	10	$61.62
3.	4	9	6	9	7	2	0	
5.	5	4	5	3	0	1	2	
6.	8	0	9	8	5	3	4	
8.	6	8	0	6	8	0	3	
9.	5	4	2	1	6	7	3	
11.	9	6	4	9	5	3	1	
12.	2	8	8	1	3	0	1	
13.	9	2	4	5	1	9	5	
14.	9	6	7	8	5	4	2	
16.	5	6	8	1	7	1	0	

Down

	1¢	5¢	10¢	25¢	50¢	$1.00	$5.00	Total
2.	5	8	6	0	9	4	4	
4.	1	4	1	7	6	2	7	
5.	0	8	8	1	9	3	2	
7.	8	3	8	2	9	1	9	
9.	6	7	5	3	3	4	3	
10.	2	7	5	2	4	5	0	
11.	4	3	8	2	7	3	2	
13.	5	9	6	7	4	3	6	
15.	6	2	6	1	9	10	7	

Puzzle 28 ᕯ ᕯ ᕯ ᕯ ᕯ ᕯ ᕯ ᕯ ᕯ ᕯ ᕯ ᕯ ᕯ

Money "Cents" *(cont.)*

See page 39 for the Across and Down clues.

1. $6 | 1 | .6 | **2.** 2

Puzzle 29 ə ☺ ə ə ☺ ə ə ☺ ə ə ☺ ə ə ə ☺ ə ☺ ə

Tax Time

Use the chart on page 42 and a calculator to figure out the tax for each amount of income. Write that amount in the number puzzle on page 42. Be sure to include the dollar signs in the puzzle. See #2 Across. It has been done for you.

Across

2. Ron earned $81,940. How much tax did he pay? _____ $20,485 _____

5. Howard earned $49,296. How much tax did he pay? _____

7. William earned $29,320. How much tax did he pay? _____

8. Eddie earned $3,600. How much tax did he pay? _____

10. Sean earned $51,500. How much tax did he pay? _____

12. Scott earned $50,792. How much tax did he pay? _____

14. Jackie earned $52,680. How much tax did she pay? _____

15. Brent earned $17,020. How much tax did he pay? _____

17. Lucy earned $94,000. How much tax did she pay? _____

Down

1. James earned $1,300. How much tax did he pay? _____

3. Gracie earned $8,720. How much tax did she pay? _____

4. Bryan earned $34,524. How much tax did he pay? _____

6. Arthur earned $17,700. How much tax did he pay? _____

7. Eva earned $26,040. How much tax did she pay? _____

9. Alice earned $33,580. How much tax did she pay? _____

11. Matt earned $8,110. How much tax did he pay? _____

12. Gloria earned $41,432. How much tax did she pay? _____

13. Lea earned $9,880. How much tax did she pay? _____

15. Tommy earned $18,900. How much tax did he pay? _____

16. Elise earned $7,240. How much tax did she pay? _____

Puzzle 29

Tax Time *(cont.)*

See page 41 for the Across and Down clues.

Income Tax Table

Earned Income	Tax Rate	Earned Income	Tax Rate
Less than $5,000	7%	$20,000-$24,999	18%
$5,000-$9,999	10%	$25,000-$29,999	20%
$10,000-$14,999	12%	$30,000 or More	25%
$15,000-$19,999	15%		

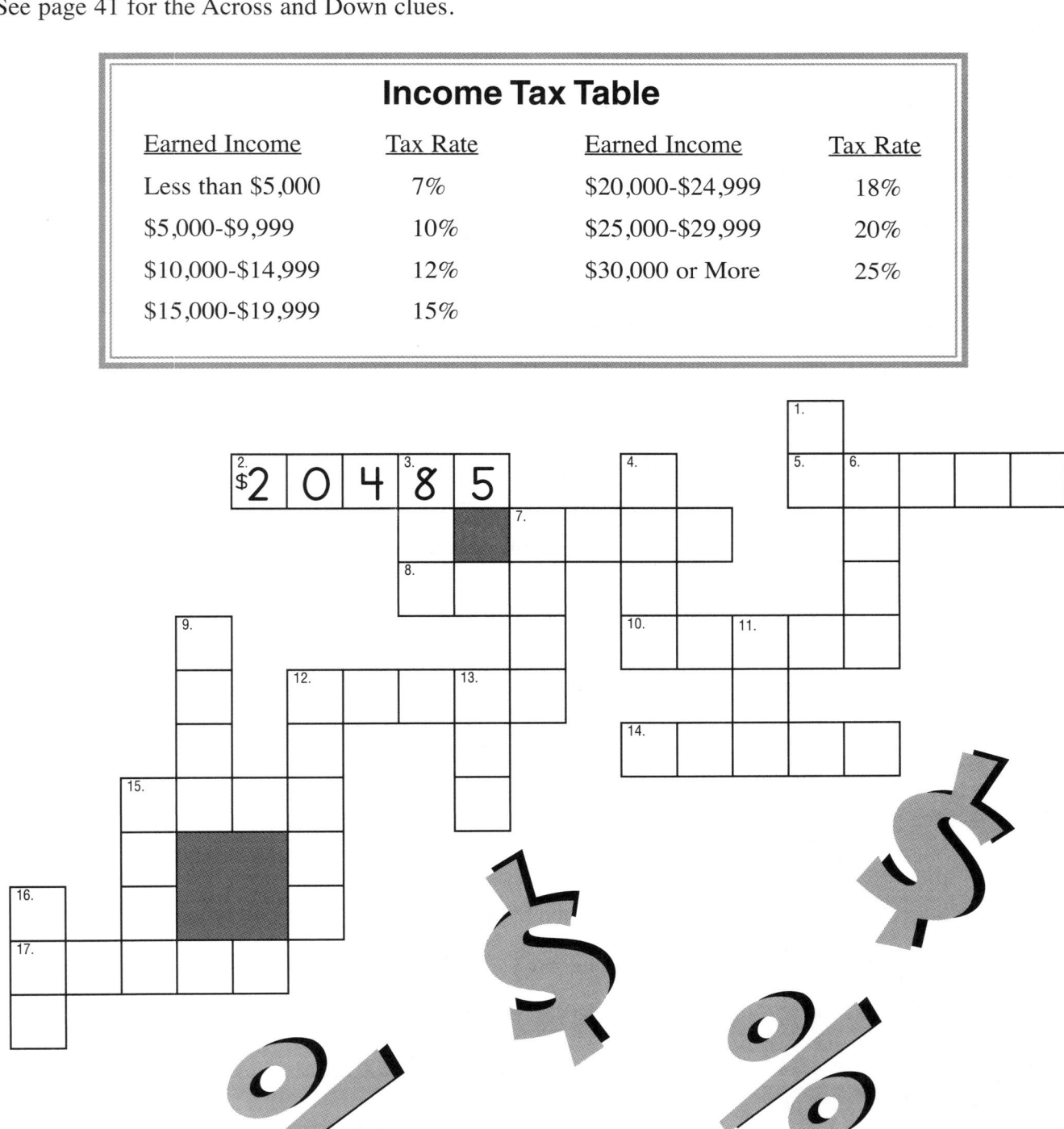

Puzzle 30

What's the Amount?

Find the amount for each problem. Write each answer in the number puzzle.

Across

1. $\frac{1}{2}$ of 54 packages = _____ packages

2. $\frac{2}{4}$ of 36 customers = _____ customers

3. $\frac{5}{10}$ of 30 letters = _____ letters

4. $\frac{8}{16}$ of 92 zip codes = _____ zip codes

5. $\frac{4}{10}$ of 70 postage stamps = _____ postage stamps

6. $\frac{8}{10}$ of 100 apartments = _____ apartments

7. $\frac{2}{5}$ of 35 mail orders = _____ mail orders

8. $\frac{3}{4}$ of 16 questions = _____ questions

9. $\frac{1}{4}$ of 64 mail trucks = _____ mail trucks

10. $\frac{3}{5}$ of 20 mailboxes = _____ mailboxes

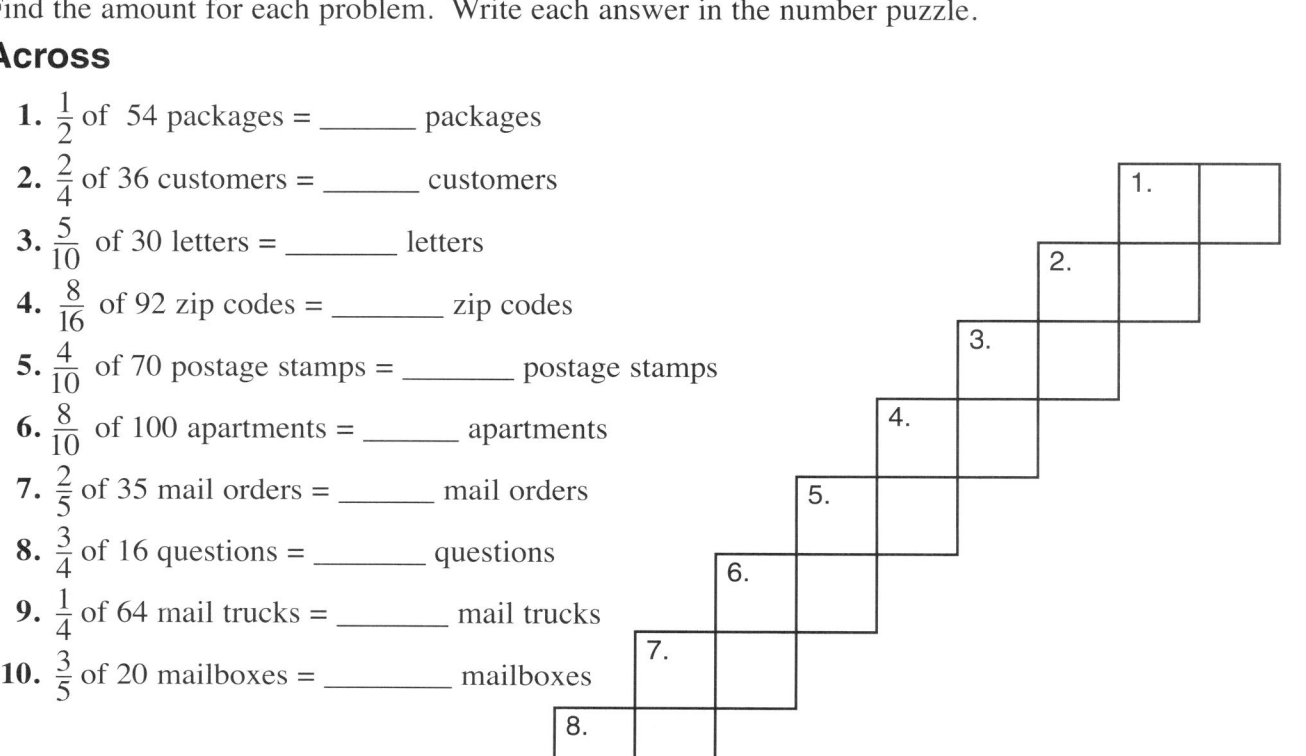

Down

1. $\frac{7}{10}$ of 40 envelopes = _____ envelopes

2. $\frac{1}{5}$ of 75 postcards = _____ postcards

3. $\frac{2}{8}$ of 64 address stamps = _____ address stamps

4. $\frac{6}{10}$ of 80 packages = _____ packages

5. $\frac{5}{8}$ of 32 magazines = _____ magazines

6. $\frac{7}{8}$ of 96 boxes = _____ boxes

7. $\frac{3}{8}$ of 32 rolls of stamps = _____ rolls of stamps

8. $\frac{8}{10}$ of 20 collectibles = _____ collectibles

9. $\frac{4}{8}$ of 24 windows = _____ windows

10. $\frac{6}{8}$ of 16 employees = _____ employees

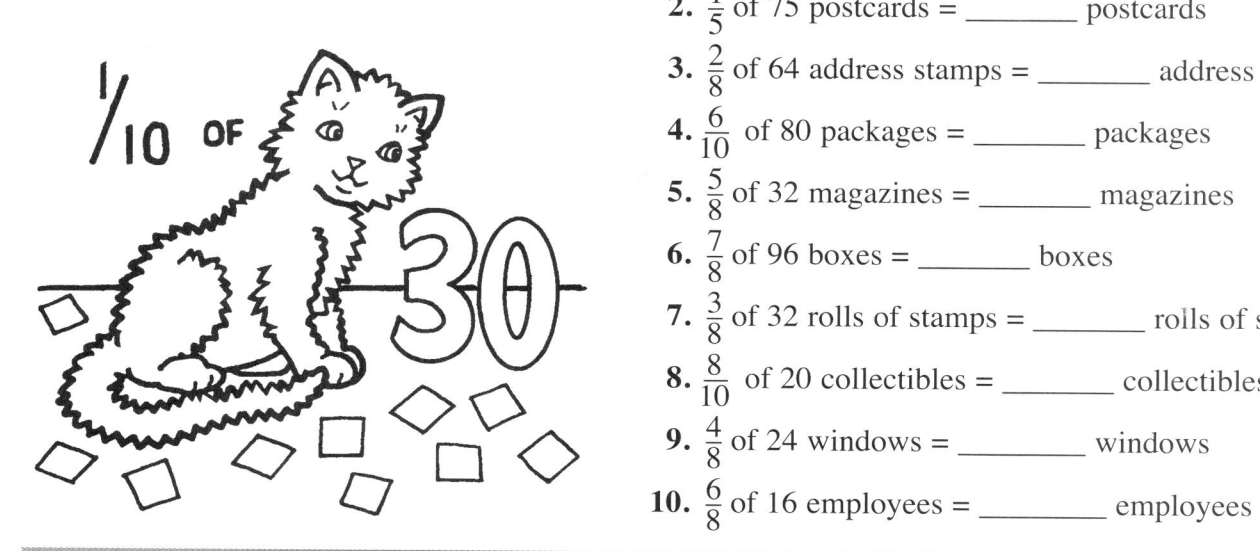

Answer Key

Puzzle 1 Page 4

Puzzle 2 Page 5

Puzzle 3 Page 6

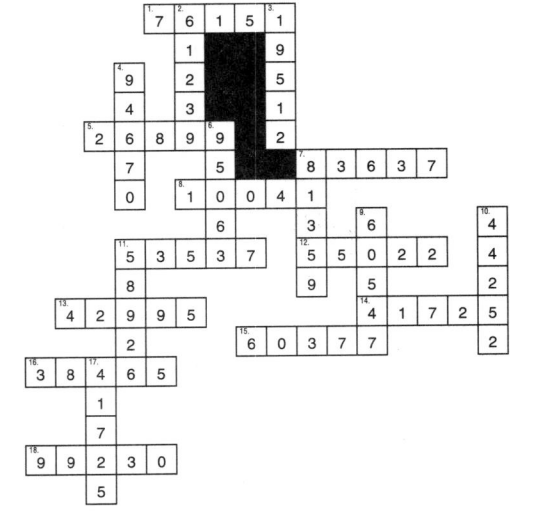

Puzzle 4 Page 7

Puzzle 5 Page 9

Puzzle 6 Page 11

Answer Key

Puzzle 7 Page 13

Puzzle 10 Page 17

Puzzle 8 Page 15

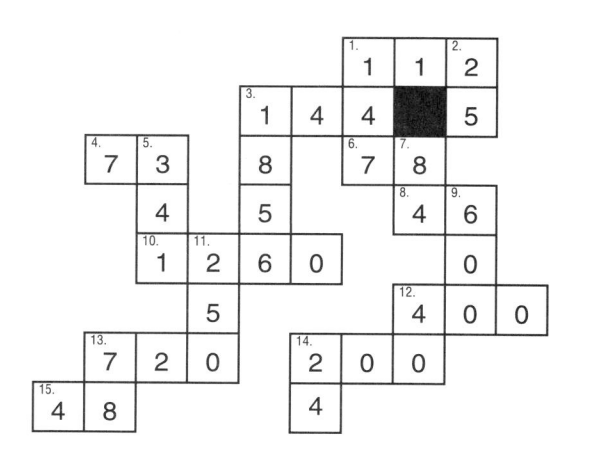

Puzzle 11 Page 18

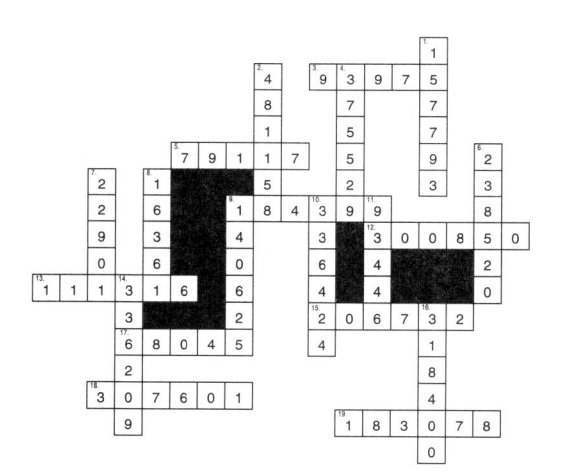

Puzzle 9 Page 16

Puzzle 12 Page 19

Answer Key

Puzzle 13 Page 20

Puzzle 14 Page 21

Puzzle 15 Page 22

Puzzle 16 Page 23

Puzzle 17 Page 24

Puzzle 18 Page 25

Answer Key

Puzzle 19 Page 26

Puzzle 20 Page 27

Puzzle 21 Page 28

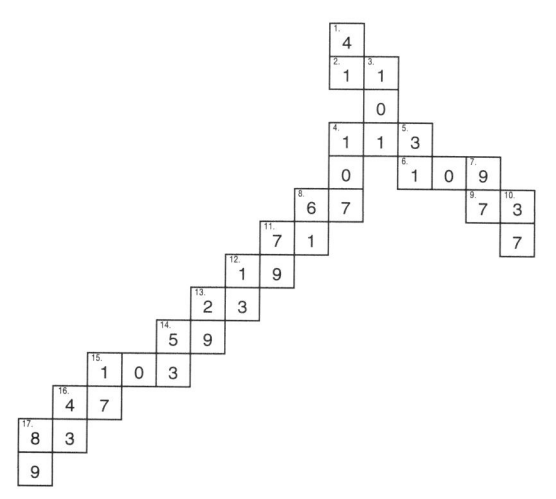

Puzzle 22 Page 29

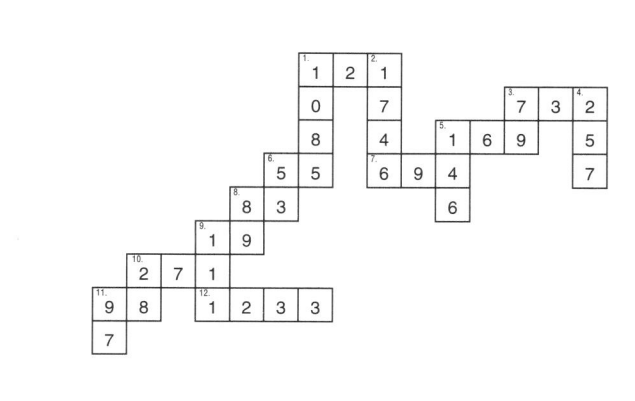

Puzzle 23 Page 30

Puzzle 24 Page 32

Answer Key

Puzzle 25 Page 34

Puzzle 26 Page 36

Puzzle 27 Page 38

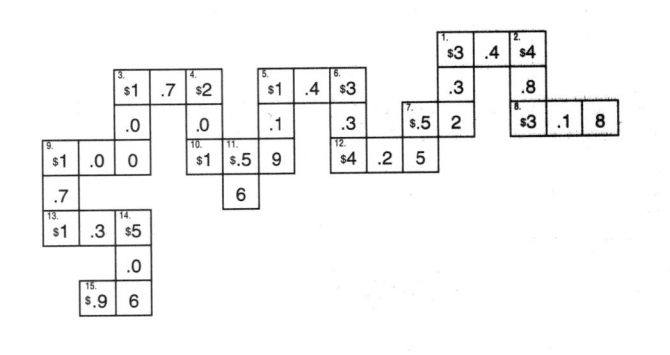

Puzzle 28 Page 40

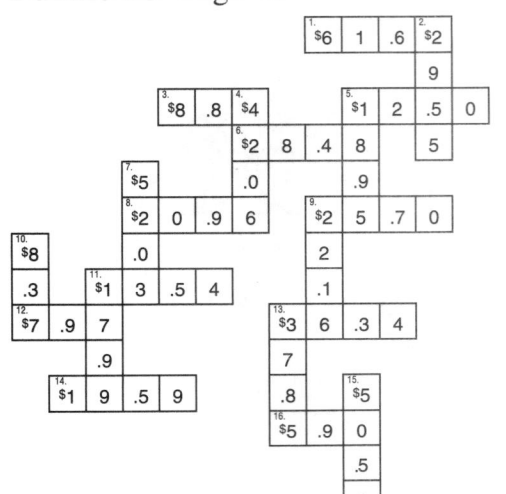

Puzzle 29 Page 42

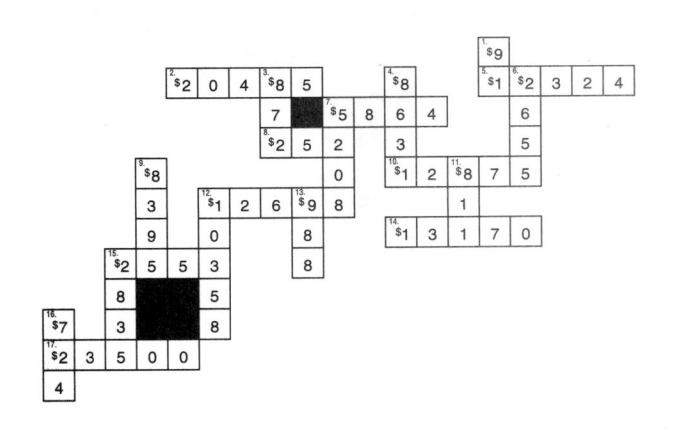

Puzzle 30 Page 43

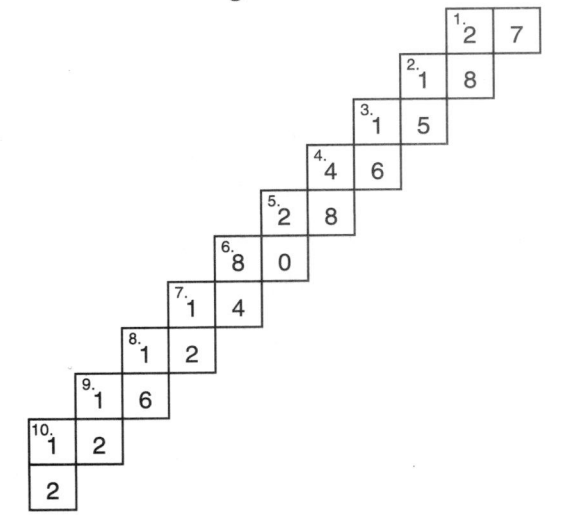